TERROR
IN WICHITA

A True Story of One Woman's Courage and Her Will to Live

PAUL F. CARANCI

Visit our website at www.StillwaterPress.com for more information.

First Stillwater River Publications Edition

ISBN-13: 978-1-950-33991-4

1 2 3 4 5 6 7 8 9

Written by Paul F. Caranci
Cover design by Emma St. Jean
Published by Stillwater River Publications, Pawtucket, RI, USA.

For Margie,
our children, Heather and Matthew,
and our grandchildren, Matthew Jr., Jacob,
Vincent and Casey

Acknowledgements

As always, I would like to acknowledge my family for their patience, encouragement and support during my writing process, and Steve and Dawn Porter at Stillwater River Publications for their guidance and valuable input throughout the publishing process. I also want to acknowledge and thank television and film producer Zig Gauthier of Red Varden Studios for his collaboration on this project. Finally, I wish to thank Lucille Boss for proofreading the manuscript and taking the time to offer her suggestions. Her attention to the smallest detail certainly helped improve the flow of the story.

Table of Contents

Preface

Violent crime is all around us. It occurs daily, is not geographically contained to certain areas, and does not take place only at night. It does not always happen only to those who look for it, as is often said, and its victims are not defined by age, gender, or race. There is no single or obvious motive and there is oftentimes no remorse on the part of the perpetrator. We never know who the next victim will be, and we never know who might decide to execute the unconscionable acts. Many times, the selected victim is random, while at other times, the target is a close friend or relative of the offender.

Regardless of the motive, venue or target, in 2018 there were more than forty-two murders committed each and every day in the United States alone. Those are lives lost for no good or apparent reason. Some of the victims were attacked because of greed, some because of lust and some simply for being in the wrong place at the wrong time.

Terror in Wichita: A True Story of One Woman's Courage and Her Will to Live, is a story of two siblings who committed egregious acts of horror on innocent people who fell victim to all the referenced scenarios. The story, an hour-by-hour, day-to-day accounting of the events, will bring you into the minds of the killers and provide an opportunity to see how and why their victims were chosen. It will bond you with the victims causing you to live and relive the horrific events of those nine days in December. It will introduce you to a woman of extraordinary courage: one who refused to become just another casualty at the hands of two "soulless monsters" whose greed, lust and total disregard for the value of human life led to one of the most heinous and ghastly string of attacks and murders imaginable.

Throughout this book the victim, turned heroine, is referred to simply as HG to protect her true identity,

The Major Characters

Adams, Tronda – Jonathan Carr's girlfriend.

Beck, Jean – A neighbor of Jason Befort, Brad Heyka and Aaron Sander.

Befort, Jason – HG's boyfriend who was beaten, robbed and murdered by the Carr brothers in December 2000.

Buggs, Dawnyieka – The neighbor who called police after Tondra Adams and Toni Greene recognized Reginald Carr as the person police sought in connection with the quadruple murder.

Carr, Jonathan D. – One of the two brothers involved in the robbery, rape and murder of several people in December 2000.

Carr, Reginald D. – One of the two brothers involved in the robbery, rape and murder of several people in December 2000.

Clark, Paul – The trial judge in the trial of Reginald and Jonathan Carr.

Cunningham, Mark – The forensic psychologist who testified at the Carr brothers' trial.

Dean, Michael – The Wichita Police Officer first to arrive at the crime scene at 12727 Birchwood Drive.

Donley, Stefanie – Reginald Carr's girlfriend.

Dudley, Mary – The Sedgwick County Coroner.

Evans, Ron – The attorney who assisted in Jonathan Carr's defense.

HG – The survivor of the rape and attempted murder committed by the Carr brothers in December 2000. She was the girlfriend of Jason Befort. She is identified in this book only as HG to protect her identity.

Harding, Phyllis – Reginald and Jonathan Carr's maternal aunt.

Heyka, Brad - One of the victims beaten and murdered by the Carr brothers in December 2000.

Hoofer, John – The Wichita Police Sergeant who responded to the crime scene at 12727 Birchwood Drive.

Foulston, Nola – The District Attorney who led the prosecution of the Carr brothers.

Greene, Toni – The mother of Tronda Adams.

Greeno, Jay – The lead attorney for Reginald Carr.

Johnson, Steve – The owner of the house to which HG ran on December 15, 2000.

Kelley, Anna – Linda Ann Walenta's neighbor.

Manna, Mark – The lead attorney for Jonathan Carr.

Muller, Heather – One of the victims raped and murdered by the Carr brothers in December 2000.

Muller, Lois – Heather Muller's mother.

Nikki – HG's pet schnauzer.

Nsangalufu, Riwa Obel – A resident who cooperated with police after helping Reginald Carr move a stolen television into Tronda Adams' apartment building.

Parker, Kim – The Chief Deputy Attorney who assisted Nola Foulston in the prosecution of Reginald and Jonathan Carr.

Porter, Scott – The trauma surgeon who testified in court at the Carr trial.

Sander, Aaron – A victim beaten and murdered by the Carr brothers in December 2000.

Schreiber, Andrew – The first victim and survivor of the Carr brothers attack in December 2000.

Siwek, Barbara – The Wichita Police Department's Crime Scene Investigator.

Taylor, Christian – Called police after spotting Reginald Carr in the parking lot of his apartment complex.

Wachtel, Val – The attorney who assisted in Reginald Carr's defense.

Walenta, Linda Ann – The first murder victim of the Carr brothers in December 2000.

Chapter 1
Massacre in the Snow

Friday, December 15, 2000
Approximately 2:07 A.M.

The soccer field at 29 North was still under construction when Aaron Sander's white Honda Accord turned off Greenwich Avenue and onto the darkened roadway that led to the field. The vehicle rolled close to the median of the long stretch of road in the rural area before coming to a complete stop and it was closely followed by a 1999 silver Dodge Dakota pickup truck which pulled along the side of it.

On this morning, however, Aaron wasn't driving his Honda. It was, rather, Reginald D. Carr, a tall, heavy-set black man, who stepped out from behind the wheel. He was still holding the small, silver, semi-automatic handgun that he used to force Heather Muller into the passenger seat some twenty minutes earlier.

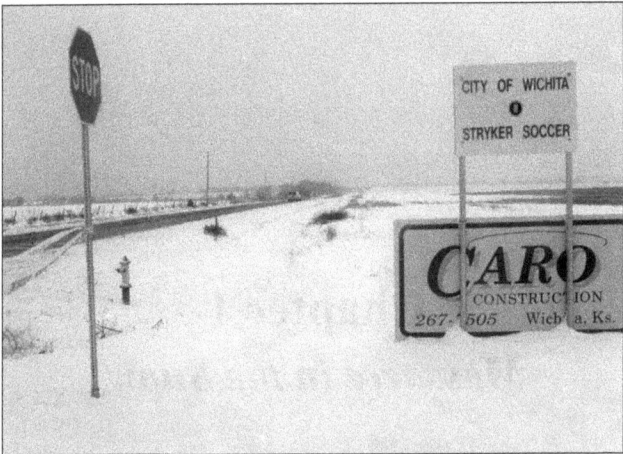

Crime scene photo showing the entrance of the soccer field where the Carr brothers concluded their nine-day crime spree.

Jonathan D. Carr exited the driver's seat of the pick-up truck holding a similar-style weapon and the two brothers spoke for a few minutes before Jonathan waved his gun to motion for his passenger, twenty-five-year-old HG, to exit that vehicle. Her shoulder-length brown hair was held tightly to the top of her head by a multicolored plastic clip. Her bare feet landed in the icy snow as she stepped from the pickup truck and was immediately ordered to sit in the driver's seat of the Accord while Heather remained in the passenger seat. The two, each naked except for a sweater they grabbed before being forced into the vehicles, sat in silence as one of their captors walked around to the rear of the Honda. Using the key, he opened the trunk, ordering the three completely naked men out. They had been stuffed into the tiny confines of the Accord's trunk at the same time that Heather and HG were taken. Aaron Sander, Brad Heyka and Jason Befort, climbed out from the trunk and were ordered at gunpoint to walk toward the front of the car.

Approximately 2:13 A.M.

It was no longer snowing, but the few inches that had fallen late the night before felt very cold on the captives' bare feet. It was a bitter seventeen degrees

Aaron Sander's Honda Accord parked at the site of the execution.

Fahrenheit and all five hostages had been naked since first being taken captive some four hours prior. When the three men reached the front of the Honda, they were told to kneel in the snow with their backs to the car. They knelt in plain view of the two women: first Aaron, then Brad and Jason. HG turned to Heather. "They're going to shoot us,"[1] she said. Just as the words left her lips, the women were directed out of the car and ordered to kneel with the men. Heather knelt to the left of Aaron, a good friend she had at one time dated. HG took a position to the right of her boyfriend Jason. He was, in reality, much more than her boyfriend. The two were very much in love and, unbeknownst to HG, Jason had purchased a diamond ring and planned to propose to her on Christmas day.

Approximately 2:16 A.M.

Reginald and his younger brother Jonathan walked behind their kneeling prisoners and one-by-one, began to fire a bullet into the back of each of their bowed heads. There was no discussion, no remorse. Just the premeditated, coldblooded execution of five young innocent people. The shooter started from the left firing the first bullet directly into the head of Heather. HG heard the gun blast. She also heard Aaron, a voice she knew very well, pleading. "Please, no, sir. Please."[2]

The bodies of Heather Muller, Aaron Sander, Brad Hayka and Jason Befort lie in the snow where they were executed by the Carr brothers.

Then the gun went off again, and then two more times all in rapid succession. With four of her friends already face down in the snow, HG was next in line. She heard the gun blast and could feel the impact of the bullet on the back of her head. Her vision blurred to a shade of gray, though she could see white stars, "like what they illustrate in a cartoon when someone gets bonked on the head ...or what you see when you close your eyes real fast."[3] She didn't fall forward into the snow as the others had. She was still conscious when she felt the hard kick of a boot hit her squarely in the back. The force of the blow knocked her forward, but she had the presence of mind to turn her head slightly so she wouldn't be face-down in the snow. She knew she would be dead soon but hoped to live long enough to identify her murderers.

HG heard the sounds of two slamming truck doors and the roar of the truck engine as the Carr brothers turned the key in the ignition of the Dakota. She then felt the weight of the truck as it rolled over her ice-cold body. It had, in fact, run over all five of the victims as it raced to leave the scene.

Tire tracks left from the vehicles the Carr brothers used to enter and escape from the soccer field.

Incredibly, HG was still conscious but decided to play dead hoping to hasten the executioners' exit. She heard the truck move to the west and then stop. She was certain the two men were coming back to run over her and her friends again and she braced herself for the impact, but it never came. Instead, the truck just raced right past them and departed the area. She waited until she could no longer hear any sound of the engine and then, without moving her body, turned her head in time to see the truck pulling out of the road in a southerly direction on Greenwich Avenue. As the kidnapping murderers approached an intersection, one of the brothers tossed the gun used in the shootings out the window of the truck.

When HG could no longer see the truck's red taillights, she got up and looked at her companions. They were all lying face down in the snow. She looked at Jason and rolled him over. Blood was squirting from his head and dripping from his eyes. HG took off her sweater, the only article of clothing she had, and tied it around his head like a tourniquet, hoping to stop the bleeding. She then went to each of the others, calling their names as she did. No one responded and their bodies were lifeless. HG looked around for a place to run for help and noticed lights to the west which she recognized as a small airport. Thinking there would be nobody there at this hour, she turned in the direction of Highway 96. There she noticed a house to the southwest that still had its white Christmas lights on. "Those people might still be awake," she silently reasoned.

Approximately 2:19 A.M.

HG was broken-hearted by the sight of her boy-friend struggling for life but couldn't focus on that now. Bleeding profusely, frightened and thinking herself near death, HG began to run, completely naked, in the direction of those lights. She avoided the road in the event that her assailants might return, choosing instead to traverse the uneven ground of the snow-covered field. The extreme cold, and the snow pinching her bare feet, made the trek unbearable and caused her to shiver uncontrollably as she ran. Each time she noticed the headlights of an approaching vehicle, three or four times in all, she dove to the ground and covered her naked body with snow thinking it might be her captors returning to the scene. "If they don't see anybody running," she thought, "they will think that everyone is where they left them."[4]

HG continued her run southwest eventually coming to a chain-link fence topped with barbed wire. Without hesitation, she climbed the fence that separated the field from Highway 96 and jumped over to the other side, ripping her skin on the shards of jagged metal as she did. She quickly crossed the road and climbed an identical fence on the other side of the highway, experiencing the agony of more torn skin in the process. HG's entire body now oozed blood. It flowed freely from her head as a result of the gunshot wound, from her shredded skin caused by the barbed wire, and from her vagina which was torn in the repeated rapes she experienced a few hours earlier. Undaunted by her injuries and driven by adrenaline, HG now had an unobstructed path to a dirt road that took her directly behind the subdivision.

ACTUAL 911 AUDIO

We got a girl that just came at our door.

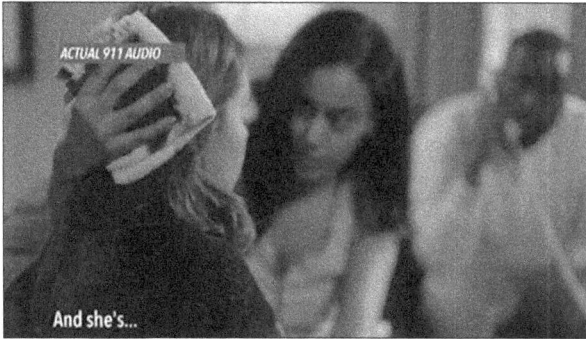

ACTUAL 911 AUDIO

And she's...

ACTUAL 911 AUDIO

naked and bleeding. And she said her friends have been shot.

ACTUAL 911 AUDIO

HG: These two men broke into our house. And they held us...

ACTUAL 911 AUDIO

and they took everything. And they executed my four friends.

Photo sequence of a dramatization from the television show Killer Siblings depicting the actual 911 call transcript made by Steve Johnson after a naked and bleeding HG showed up at his door in the early morning hours of December 15, 2000.

HG's fear and paranoia convinced her that an approaching vehicle contained her assailants. Reacting accordingly, she gathered all of her remaining strength and ran toward the subdivision as fast as her legs would carry her. The Christmas lights were still a block or so away, but HG saw another house, a white one, also with Christmas light ablaze. It was even closer.

She had completed the more than one-mile-long trek in less than 20 minutes, but she was not yet done. She ran around to the front door of the white house, feeling a small sense of relief as she ran to the security of the front porch. She rang the bell and incessantly pounded her fist hard against the wooden door. She didn't stop pounding when she saw a young couple peer from behind a long panel of glass. She didn't stop until they opened the door to let her in. "Call 911,"[5] she shouted.

2:37 A.M.

Steve Johnson and his girlfriend Kim had been living together for a relatively short time when they opened the door of their home in the 2400 block of Regency Lakes Court to the naked, bloodied, and shivering woman. As soon as she entered, HG began to relay the horrific events of the past several hours. Fearing she might die at any moment she wanted her story told so that her description of the killers could be relayed to police.

Steve could not wait to hear her entire story, however. He called 911 almost immediately as his wife retrieved a blanket which she used to cover the hysterical woman. Steve began to convey HG's story, and the minute details that she was giving him, to the dispatcher. The exhausted woman was understandably excited and talking far too fast and sobbing far too heavily for Steve to adequately understand and transmit the information. Consequently, he handed the phone to HG so she could describe the events of the evening directly to the dispatcher. At one point she lost consciousness, but after being revived, she was able to provide to the dispatcher a fairly accurate description of the events of both the late evening and the early morning. She described in extraordinary detail what the men did, where they did it, what they were driving and how she got away. Perhaps even more significantly, she was able to provide a remarkably accurate description of the two men who attacked her and killed her friends.

Chapter 2
A Troubled Past

Approximately 1978 - 2000

If it is true that a dysfunctional family, abuse, and exposure to drugs and violence will increase the probability of a life of tribulation, then perhaps Reginald and Jonathan Carr were doomed from the start. An examination of a list of risk factors that might lead to criminal behavior would reveal that the Carrs experienced almost all of them.

By all accounts, the brothers had a dreadful childhood. They were abandoned by their father, sexually abused by their stepfather, and beaten by their mother. By the age of six, older brother Reginald was fondling girls that his mother babysat in her home. By age seven, he began having frequent sexual intercourse with his female cousin. Later, he obtained pornographic photographs of his mother, images he kept hidden for years. By age eleven, his uncles had given him alcohol and he was holding drugs for pushers. By age thirteen, he was a full-fledged drug dealer with his own mother as a customer. She would disappear for days at a time, leaving Reginald and his brother with abusive relatives. At age sixteen, when many of his school-aged peers were excited about taking their drivers' license exam, Reginald was out getting drunk.

Reginald (L) and Jonathan Carr (R)

Reginald and Jonathan frequently shot animals with BB guns, and when they could find no animals to shoot, they took shots at each other. In fact, one BB that lodged in Reginald's head from one such encounter with his sibling was never removed. Whenever the brothers were punished, they were forced to strip naked and whipped with belts or electrical cords while other siblings held them down.

Reginald attended eight different schools between kindergarten and eighth grade. In eighth grade, he was suspended from school for sexually harassing his teacher. By age thirteen, he was a member of a gang, which to him was reminiscent of a gang in which one of his cousins was killed after being shot in the head.

High school was no better. During his freshman year he accrued thirty-two absences and twenty-one detentions and suspensions. He was about to be expelled for beating up another student when he decided to quit school. He obtained his GED while on criminal probation, but found himself in prison at age eighteen.

Jonathan, two years Reginald's junior, didn't fare much better. He lived with his Aunt Phyllis Harding when he was seven. Harding, their mother's sister, resided in Brownsville, Texas, where she worked as a pediatrician. Shortly after taking him in, however, Harding and Jonathan moved to Dodge City, Kansas. She remembers Jonathan as always full of rage and unable to hold a steady job for more than a few months at a time. Dodge City was not the best place for a child to grow. In fact, with a crime rate 28% higher than other parts of the country, it wasn't even a particularly pleasant place to live even as an adult.

The Carr brothers, Jonathan (L) and Reginald (R)

It was during these formative years the Carr brothers grew to regard human relationships as inconsequential and lives as disposable. They were damaged goods. Many people have less than idyllic childhoods: many of them overcome the abuse and become productive members of society. Reginald and Jonathan Carr were not among them.

Chapter 3
The Carrs' Reign of Terror Begins

It would not appear that murder was a motive. Nor would it seem that race or hate played a part in their actions despite the fact that all of their victims were white. Rather, greed, precariously coupled with a deliberate disregard for human life–a quality that had been inculcated over the course of many years–figured to be the Carr brothers' impetus. Motive aside, however, the brothers were about to begin a crime spree that would draw national attention, become the source of protests and discord within communities, and generate charges and countercharges of racism and cover-up.

Their plan was as ill-conceived as it was executed. The original plan was to follow people in expensive vehicles, carjack them, force them to empty their bank accounts using local ATMs, and then release the victims unharmed. Things did not go as planned.

Thursday, December 7, 2000
10:50 P.M.

For twenty-three-year-old Andrew Schreiber, life was wonderful. As a sports enthusiast, he was lucky enough to work as an assistant baseball coach at Newman University in Wichita, Kansas. He had loved baseball ever since he could walk and preferred to catch so he could be involved in every play and every pitch of nearly every game. When not playing baseball, the six-foot tall, blond-haired, blue-eyed Schreiber could frequently be found on the golf course.

At about 10:45 on the evening of December 7th, Andrew arrived at the Kum & Go convenience store at 21st and Woodlawn. He made a small purchase and walked back to his SUV, a 1998 Ford Expedition, which was parked in a lot on the side of the building. He took his seat behind the wheel, but before he could turn the key in the ignition, he was approached by Reginald Carr. In his hand, Reginald held a small, black, semi-automatic handgun palm down. Carr held the gun barrel to the window of the driver's door and ordered Schreiber to move over to the front passenger seat. As Schreiber complied, Reginald climbed into the driver's seat and struck Schreiber on the back of the head with his gun.

"Hurry up,"[6] Carr ordered. Reginald then backed the SUV out of the parking lot and drove away. "Do you have any money?"[7] Reginald demanded. Schreiber handed him his wallet, which contained some cash, his credit cards and other personal effects.

Andrew Schreiber was kidnapped & robbed at gunpoint by the Carr Brothers on December 7, 2000. Though beaten, he was lucky enough to survive the attack.

The carjacker pulled into a nearby alley where Reginald's brother Jonathan jumped into the passenger seat, pushing Schreiber into the middle position of the rear seat. He was barely in position when Jonathan leaned over and struck him on the head with his gun barking, "Don't look at me."[8] One of the brothers asked if Schreiber had an ATM card adding, "Someone who drives a car like this [the Expedition] must have money."[9] Schreiber responded in the affirmative and Reginald returned his wallet instructing Schreiber to retrieve the card from it. He did so and handed the wallet back to his attacker.

Driving to a bank, Reginald pulled up to the ATM, allowing Schreiber to access it through the rear passenger window. With Jonathan's gun to his head, Schreiber

withdrew the $300.00 maximum and the gunman or-
dered him to hand the cash and receipt over his shoulder
without looking at him. Jonathan grabbed both, and
scanning the receipt, noticed that Schreiber still had
money in his account., "We are not done yet,"[10] he said.

Reginald drove to a second ATM, while Jonathan
continued to point the gun at Schreiber's head. Again,
the victim withdrew the maximum of $300.00 and
handed over both the cash and the receipt. After determining that money still remained in the account, the carjackers repeated they were not yet done. At a third ATM,
Schreiber's request for $300.00 was denied, but he was
able to withdraw $200.00, which he handed to Jonathan
along with the receipt, as he had done before. Looking at
the receipt, Jonathan said with a laugh, "We're going to
leave you with $8.00 and some change,"[11] while still
pointing his gun at Schreiber's head.

Reginald drove from the bank, traveling north of
the convenience store and then west on Highway 96.
While in-route, the carjackers ordered Schreiber to remove all his jewelry and give it to them. Obediently, he
began to remove his silver Guess watch with a blue
face, turning his head as he did. He felt the punishing
blow of the gun slam against his head a third time as
Jonathan yelled, "I told you not to look at us."[12]

The conversation between the gunmen now turned
to the possibility of dropping Schreiber off on a dirt

road. Several roads they passed were determined unsuitable because they were not remote enough for their purposes. Schreiber wondered what that purpose was as he sat silently in the rear seat of the SUV. The brothers also spoke about the Expedition and Jonathan noted how much he liked it saying he wanted one. Then, perhaps more as a way of controlling and alarming his victim, Jonathan said that he was going to take Schreiber's pants and shoes when they dropped him off, because it was so cold outside. The thought of it made Jonathan laugh with amusement at his own remark.

After driving aimlessly, Reginald eventually ended up back in town, stopping at a car wash near the Windsor at Woodgate Apartments on East 21st Street. There, Jonathan and Schreiber changed positions a few times, with Jonathan finally instructing Schreiber to lie face down on the floor in front of the rear seat. Reginald thought it wise for Jonathan to get his own car, so shortly after leaving the car wash, Reginald drove to the original meeting spot and Jonathan exited the vehicle reminding Reginald "to be sure to wipe down the Expedition."[13]

Jonathan got into his own vehicle and both men drove away with Jonathan in the lead. After another ten or fifteen minutes, the vehicles departed the paved road and came to a stop on a dirt road. Reginald turned the engine off, removed the keys from the ignition and wiped the Expedition clean. He exited the vehicle and spoke to Jonathan about whether or not they should leave Schreiber with the keys. Eventually, Reginald said to Schreiber, who was still face down on the back floor of the Expedition, that they would leave the keys in the street. "Do you have a spare tire?" he asked Schreiber. Upon learning that he did, Reginald shot three times into one of the rear tires of the Expedition instructing Schreiber to "wait 20 minutes before leaving the scene."[14]

Andrew Schreiber's 1998 Ford Expedition showing the tire that was shot out by his kidnappers during his ordeal.

Schreiber heard the two men get into the other car and drive away. He peeked out the window and "saw the receding square taillights of the other car."[15] He then exited the vehicle, found his keys in the street, and managed to drive all the way home with the flat tire. That's when he called 911. Schreiber survived the ordeal but was badly shaken by the experience and hurting from the repeated blows to the head. Though he would never be the same, he was grateful to still be alive.

Monday, December 11, 2000
Approximately 9:20 P.M.

Four days after their successful carjacking, kidnapping, and robbery of Schreiber, and apparently emboldened by their success, the brothers approached a fifty-five-year-old red-headed musician by the name of Linda Ann Walenta, known to her friends as Ann. The brothers had the expectation of carjacking her as well, but their plans would not be executed as smoothly this time.

Ann Walenta, the first murder victim of the Carr brothers, was shot three times on December 11, 2000. She died from her wounds on January 2, 2001, but not before providing police with a description of the shooter.

With youthful looks that betrayed her age, the fair-skinned woman was a cellist and librarian with the Wichita Symphony Orchestra. Along with her husband Donald, Ann had two grown children. She also had a beguiling love for classical music and enjoyed sharing its joy with others. That is what led her to work "for a group that taught classical music to young black people."[16]

At approximately 9:20 P.M. on a Monday evening, Ann waved goodbye to her orchestra mates, climbed into her 2000 GMC Yukon SUV, and began her drive home from rehearsal. As she approached the streets of her upscale East Wichita neighborhood, "she noticed a light-colored, four door-vehicle resembling a Honda, turn behind her. The car continued to follow her as she turned onto her street, a dead end with a cul-de-sac. As Walenta approached her house, she noticed that the car had stopped in front of the residence directly south of hers. And, when Walenta pulled into the driveway of her single-story home, she saw a black male emerge from the front passenger side of the light-colored car and begin walking toward the driver's side of her Yukon."[17] Now on a heightened sense of alert, Walenta left her vehicle running and decided to sit for just a moment in her SUV before exiting. For her, it was the wrong moment.

The air was cold and dry when Jonathan Carr approached her vehicle asking for help. She cautiously lowered the driver's side window only a few inches so as to hear what he was saying. Before she could respond to his plea, however, Jonathan pulled a handgun, stuck it inside the window palm down, and pointed it at her head. In a panic, Walenta tried to start the vehicle forgetting that she had left the engine running. "Don't move the car."[18] Jonathan ordered, but Walenta instinctively put the vehicle in reverse and started to back out of her driveway. That's when Jonathan began to fire. He pulled the trigger several times, shattering the window with one of three shots. The bullets entered the vehicle coming to rest in Walenta's body, one of them severing her spinal cord.

ACTUAL CRIME SCENE FOOTAGE

Actual crime scene photograph taken on the evening of December 11, 2000 in front of the home of Ann Walenta where the shooting took place.

Jonathan began to run and Walenta, still conscious, watched her assailant as he fled. While Jonathan was running toward his waiting car, Reginald started to drive it away. Walenta was paralyzed from the waist down and wasn't even sure if her shooter had made it to the waiting car prior to its leaving, but still, she wasn't taking any chances that he might have remained in the area. She fell forward on the wheel, the weight of her body pressing hard on the horn of the SUV.

Anna Kelley, Walenta's neighbor from across the street, heard the gunshots and the blare of the horn and looked outside. "She realized that the honking was coming from Walenta's Yukon, and that the Yukon's lights were flashing."[19] She opened her screen door and was about to step out when Walenta began calling to her for help. Kelley told her husband to call the police as she ran to her neighbor's car where she found Walenta, covered with blood and slumped forward in the driver's seat. With blood oozing from several places on her body, the woman told Kelley that "she had been shot by a black man with wiry hair."[20] When police and emergency responders arrived, they transported her to the hospital. Once there, Walenta was able to provide police with more details and a better description of her assailant saying that he was between five feet, nine inches and 6 feet and described his hair as long, straight, and wiry, adding that it was about shoulder length with corkscrews.

Though critical when she arrived at the hospital, Walenta's condition began to improve. She remained in the hospital for several weeks and on January 2, 2001, was being transferred to a rehabilitation facility. "On

that day, however, she suffered a pulmonary embolus–
a complication of her paralysis–and died," Though sur-
viving for three weeks, Linda Ann Walenta would be
considered the first murder victim of the Carr brothers'
greed and selfishness, manifested just three weeks before Christmas. She would not be their last.

Chapter 4
Horror in Wichita

Thursday, December 14, 2000
Approximately 8:00 P.M.

HG was happy with just about every aspect of her life. The twenty-five-year-old, five feet, four-inch tall teacher at the Rose Hill Elementary School didn't always want to be an educator, though "she always knew she wanted to help people in some capacity."[21] Initially she thought about a career in the medical profession, and to that end, she majored in pre-med at college. But the influence of a seventh-grade algebra teacher that she "admired and had always wanted to be like,"[22] had a profound impact on causing her to rethink her goals during her high school years.

HG had been acquainted with Jason Befort for many years and over the course of that time the two fell deeply in love. Jason, too, was a teacher. At age twenty-six, he taught science and coached junior varsity basketball at the Augusta High School, about 20 miles east of Wichita. Unbeknownst to HG, Jason had recently purchased a diamond ring which he had securely hidden away until the time was right to ask the question. In his desire to make the highly anticipated evening perfect, he had also purchased a book on how to propose. He planned on surprising HG with the ring and a request for marriage on Christmas Day.

Jason Befort hoped to propose to HG Christmas Day. He was never given the chance.

Befort lived in Wichita, in the middle unit of a triplex condominium at 12727 Birchwood Drive at the intersection of 127th Street. He shared the house with two good friends from college–twenty-seven-year-old Brad Heyka and twenty-nine-year-old Aaron Sander.

Though it wasn't that unusual for HG to spend the night at Jason's place, she was still excited as she prepared to do so on this night. She tossed her overnight bag into her car and carefully placed a homemade cheesecake onto the seat. Then, picking up Nikki, the little gray schnauzer she adored, HG placed her in the car and began the trek to Birchwood Drive. It was very cold, and the snow had begun falling a few hours earlier. A great deal of snow had not been predicted, but the bitterly cold temperature, coupled with the falling snow, required that HG proceed with great caution so as not to slide on the snow and ice-slicked roads.

Approximately 8:30 P.M.

Arriving at Jason's house, HG pulled her car into the driveway, noticing that Jason's 1999 Dodge Dakota was not there. She exited her vehicle and let little Nikki

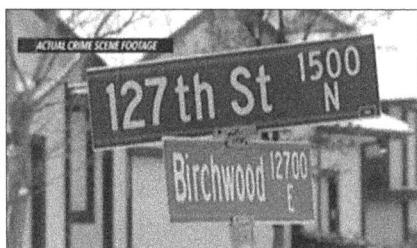

The triplex shared by Jason Befort, Aaron Sander and Brad Heyka can be seen behind the street signs.

go to the bathroom before using her own key to open the front door, leaving it unlocked behind her. She yelled hello to Aaron, who was in the kitchen, and to Brad, who was watching television in the lower level, then went to Jason's room and sat down on his bed to grade some papers while waiting for him to return from basketball practice. She had known Jason's two roommates for quite a while and they had become her friends as well.

Jason's bedroom was located at the front of the tri-plex so chances were good that HG would notice his headlights shine into the bedroom as he was driving up. The condominium, built in 1984, had a somewhat open floor plan and was a rather large 3-bed, 3 bath unit with 2,400 square feet. Adjacent to Jason's bedroom was the living room where the Christmas tree stood in front of the window in the southwest corner of the room, right by the sliding glass doors that led to the back of the house and overlooked a pond. Directly outside of Jason's bedroom, between the living room and the bedroom, was an "L-shaped" hallway with a wet bar area forming the shorter side of the "L". The bathroom was also located off the hall opposite the bar. Aaron's bedroom was right down the hall and the kitchen was off the living room. On the lower level were Brad's living room and bedroom.[23]

Front view of the triplex shared by Befort, Sander, and Heyka.

As HG reviewed her students' work, Heather Muller, Aaron Sander's former girlfriend, arrived. Heather was an attractive brunette who wore her hair in a page-boy style. She had just come from a meeting at the Catholic student center where she was planning a 50th anniversary celebration for some friends. She left the center at about 8:00 P.M. when the meeting ended. Heather was a vivacious woman loved by everyone. She had a great affinity for music and had performed in many productions both in high school and in college, including in the Wichita State University Concert Chorale in 1998-99. After college, she continued to sing in the choir at St. Paul Catholic Church.

Heather Muller and Aaron Sander had once dated. Now Aaron studied for the priesthood while Heather was very active in her church where she sang in the choir.

On this night, she was dressed in blue jeans and a denim shirt, topped with a sweater. She and Aaron Sander had once dated, but the two ended their romantic relationship when Aaron felt a calling to the priesthood. Since that time, they remained good friends and Heather even entertained her own thoughts of joining a convent. Heather seldom spent the night at the triplex, in fact, to HG's recollection, this might have been only the second time. The first time they slept separately, with Heather sleeping in Aaron's bed and Aaron spending the night on the couch downstairs. HG had no reason to think tonight's arrangement would be any different.

Upon arriving, Heather immediately made her way into the kitchen to join Aaron, who was making dinner. Though HG was acquainted with Heather, the two were not really friends and HG didn't even know her last name.

At 9:00, HG began watching *ER*, one of her favorite television shows, while continuing to grade her class papers. She knew that Jason would be home soon.

Approximately 9:15 P.M.

Shortly after *ER* began, Jason arrived home and went into his bedroom to change out of his basketball clothes. He kissed his girlfriend and the two talked for a bit while Jason put on his sleep garb, the usual T-shirt and athletic shorts. Then, as was typical, he went downstairs to join Brad in the living room. The two spent a great deal of their free time in the lower-level living room watching Brad's 52-inch large-screen television. HG didn't mind that he did so, after all, she was busy and thought the little routine was rather cute. In fact, the thought of it even brought a smile to her face.

10:00 P.M.

With another weekly episode of *ER* coming to an end, HG retreated to the downstairs living room to join Jason and Brad. She had not yet finished grading her papers, but her bedtime was fast approaching. Despite being at Jason's house, she still had to be up early the next morning for work. Normally she would be in bed between 10 and 10:30 on a work-night. Consequently, she was downstairs

Brad Heyka

with Jason and Brad for only a short time before returning to the first floor and heading toward Jason's room. On the way to the bedroom she noticed that Aaron and Heather were no longer in the kitchen and she assumed that they were probably talking somewhere else in the house. Once HG reached Jason's room, she pulled her hair back, fastened it with a plastic clip and got into bed.

Just about the same time, Brad decided that he too would call it a night though his bedroom was the only one located in the lower lever of the condo. A short time later, Jason walked up the stairs, locked the front door, turned off all the lights and went to his room for the evening. For some reason, the job of turning off all the lights had become his, perhaps because he was usually the only one of the roommates that remembered to do it. In any case, ensuring that the lights were off was of greater concern to Jason because the porch light was directly outside his bedroom window and his room was not darkened unless that light was off.

Approximately 11:00 P.M. to 11:45 P.M.

Jean Beck, one of Jason's neighbors, was returning from a night at The Grape, a restaurant at Central and Rock Road in Wichita, just a short distance from Walenta's home. Beck had gone to The Grape right after work. At about 10:45 P.M she walked out of the building, got into her 2000 BMW 323, and began the drive home. As she neared her house, she noticed a tan Toyota four-door vehicle behind her. When she turned off 13th Street the car followed her causing Beck to call her daughter asking her to open the garage door at their condo at 12725 Birchwood Drive – directly adjacent to Jason's unit. As a precaution, Beck remained in her vehicle until she saw the Toyota pass her home and head back toward 13th Street. Only then did she exit the BMW and enter her home.

The tan Toyota returned, however, about 10 minutes later. Two black men exited the vehicle and walked onto the porch of Jason, Brad and Aaron's condo. It is quite possible that they thought they were at the door of Jean Beck, the woman in the fancy car that they had followed. Regardless, they knocked on the door. Within seconds the porch light was flipped on and Aaron stood in the doorway. The two brothers forced their way into the condo with Aaron at gunpoint.

Jason became upset as his room illuminated from the porch light and mumbled "Don't tell me I have to get up and turn the lights off again." It was just then that HG heard Aaron talking to somebody in the hallway. She presumed it to be Heather, though she couldn't hear the other voice. She leaned up to see the clock, but with Jason's head partially in the way, could see only the first two numbers of the digital clock. They read "11".

Just then Jason's bedroom door burst open. Thinking it was Aaron, HG turned over trying to go back to sleep... that is until she heard Jason scream. HG sprang forward and looked toward the door observing a tall black male standing in the doorway pointing a gun in their direction. Though HG did not recognize him as anyone she had ever seen before, it was Jonathan Carr. He wore a mid-length leather coat, jeans, an orange and black FUBU sweater, and black gloves. Waving a gun, the intruder approached the bed and ripped away the blanket and sheet that covered Aaron and HG. He had a rather crazy, perhaps even intimidating hairstyle. A "clumpy, spiky style with bits of hair clumped together,"[24] as HG remembered it. The hair reminded her of Buckwheat, the lovable little boy from the *Little Rascals* television show popular in the 1950s, though to the best of her recollection, Buckwheat never pointed a gun at anyone.

The Carr brothers, Reginald (L) and Jonathan (R)

The intruder appeared to HG to be in his early twenties and about 6 feet tall. A hushed discussion ensued between Jason and the intruder, but before HG could focus on what was being said, another black man appeared in the room. This one seemed equally as tall as the first though a bit thinner. He too brandished a gun and squeezing the fully dressed Aaron by the shirt, shoved him into the room and onto the bed. This gunman was Jonathan's older brother Reginald.

HG's dog Nikki, normally quite affable and friendly, began to growl and bare her teeth. "Grab your dog or we'll shoot her,"[25] one of the intruders commanded of no one in particular. HG took hold of Nikki and tried to calm her. "Who else is in the house?"[26] One of the men demanded, "and don't lie." Aaron told them that Brad was downstairs, adding under relentless questioning, "my girlfriend's in the other room."[27] One of the brothers immediately left the room and went downstairs in search of Brad.

A distant scream broke the momentary silence that ensued and within seconds, Brad was thrust into the bedroom as the same intruder, now holding a golf club, went off in search of Heather, whom he found rather quickly. The intruder led Heather into the room still dressed as she was when she first arrived.

All five friends were now held captive in Jason's rather small room illuminated only by the porch light. HG and Jason sat on the bed with Aaron at the foot of the bed. Heather sat on the floor closest to the foot of the bed and Brad was also positioned on the floor. With all housemates fully accounted for, the Carr brothers turned their attention to the location of any phones. "The phone in the kitchen," Aaron said. "You know, I already told you, just the phone in the kitchen."[28] Still, several more times, the brothers asked if there was any-one else in the house and if there were any other phones. The answers remained the same though the sit-uation was anything but stable. The intruders sounded irrational. Their voices were loud, and their questions were more like directives. Panic had started to set in, though no threats, other than about the dog, were yet made. That was about to change.

"Where's your money,"[29] the gunmen insisted. They became angry when they learned there was no cash on hand of which to speak, but quickly turned their attention to the ATM option, asking which of the five hostages had a card. All five of them raised their hands. "How much money do you have in the cards,"[30] one asked. Jason said three or four hundred, HG told them she had five hundred, Brad said he had about fifteen hundred, while Heather and Aaron had two hundred dollars each. Satisfied that there was sufficient money in the various accounts to make the evening profitable, the brothers whispered to each other for a few moments and then one of them shouted to all five captors, "Get undressed."[31] One by one, each of the five complied. As the five detainees disrobed, one of the gunmen pulled all of the clothing out of Jason's closet, and or-dered all five prisoners to sit in silence on the floor in-side it. The closet door was closed in front of them and they sat, scared and trembling in the dark.

Reginald left the room and began rummaging around the living room. He turned the living room light on and yelled, "Where's the safe? In a house this fucking nice, there ha[s] to be a safe somewhere."[32] Finding nothing, he returned to the bedroom very unhappy, and the brothers decided to get their kicks a different way. One remarked, loud enough for the captives to hear, and in very crude language, how nice it would be to watch the two women engage in sex acts together.

He opened the closet door and, using his gun as a pointer, Jonathan motioned for Heather and HG to go out to the wet bar area. The men were ordered to remain seated in the small closet. They complied as the girls stood up and exited the bedroom followed by both gun-men, one of whom remained in the doorway so he could keep an eye on the bedroom closet while still being able to enjoy what was about to unfold near the bar. The other gunman shoved the girls into the open area of the bar where he ordered the two acquaintances again, in very crude and vulgar language, to perform oral sex on each other. The girls complied. Heather got down with her back on the floor as HG slid into position so her mouth could reach Heather's vagina. After a few minutes, with the gun still pointed toward them, the girls were told to switch positions. While "Heather was performing oral sex on HG, one of the intruders hit HG's knee so that he could get a better view of what was happening."[33] The

41

gunmen watched with delight directing the woman to "suck harder"[34] when the action did not seem to satisfy them. After several minutes, he ordered the girls to penetrate each other with their fingers which they did simultaneously. This time there were calls of "do it deeper"[35] when it seemed to the brothers that the two girls were just pretending. This depravity lasted for about five or ten minutes, but it was just the beginning of a long night.

The gunman told Heather to go back to the bedroom and Brad was called out. One of the intruders reached for a T-shirt that was lying there and threw it over HG's face though it did not obscure her vision so much that she couldn't identify each of the men who was compelled to penetrate her vaginally. Brad was the first forced to have intercourse with her on the floor. He had difficulty getting an erection but tried to penetrate HG as best he could. The brothers were very upset at Brad's inability to perform and yelled some profanity towards him. Irritated with the poor showing, the captors quickly sent Brad back to the bedroom and motioned for Jason to come out. HG tried not to look through the T-shirt, but after Jason began to penetrate her with his semi-flaccid penis, one of the gunmen laughed, "That's his girl. Don't let him do it with his girl."[36] Consequently, after just a few minutes, Jason was told to return to his room and Aaron was brought out.

Aaron had been preparing himself for the priesthood and its requirement for celibacy. Accordingly, he had an even greater aversion to what was being demanded of him. He resisted. "I can't do this," he protested. "I don't want to do that."[37] "You have to,"[38] the gunmen responded. When he continued to protest, the intruder raised his gun-hand and brought it down hard, slamming the gun on the back of Aaron's head at the base of his neck causing him to cry out in pain. His scream was heard by the others in the closet, increasing their own fear and anxiety. Like the others, the circumstances prevented Aaron from getting an erection, though he did try, with limited success, to penetrate HG with his flaccid penis.

At this point, HG was ordered back to the bedroom and into the closet with Jason and Brad while Heather was pulled out and told to accompany the gunmen back to the bar area. The closet is very small, only about one foot deep by about six feet wide. Three to five people being stuffed inside created conditions that were claustrophobic at best. The closet door was closed, and the light was turned on, but the prisoners were told to remain silent, which they did.

Heather was led to Aaron by the gunmen. She knew exactly what was about to transpire as she walked the twelve feet from the closet to the door leading to the hallway and then on to the adjacent bar area. From her position in the closet, HG could hear the gunmen yelling at

43

Aaron to get an erection, but he couldn't. The assailant picked up the golf club he had carried with him from the basement when he retrieved Brad. One of the brothers used the club to strike Aaron on the back. HG could hear the contact and Aaron's screams of pain. "You have until 11:54 to get it hard,"[39] one of the gunmen bellowed. Then, looking at Jason's digital alarm clock, he started counting each minute of time from 11:52, 11:53, 11:54.

Clearly, Aaron was unable to perform under that type of pressure. Exasperated, the brothers brought Aaron back to the closet and grabbed Jason, pulling him out to the wet bar area, ordering him to have intercourse with Heather. From the distance, HG could hear Heather moaning, not from pleasure, but rather as a means of audibly quantifying the pain that she felt.

Jason returned to the closet rather quickly and Brad was taken out. He too was ordered to have intercourse with Heather, who would occasionally still release moans of pain. Throughout the entire time of the sexual assaults, the gunmen shouted obscenities as they prodded the unwilling participants on.

Approximately 11:45 P.M. Thursday, December 14, 2000 to 1:30 A.M Friday, December 15, 2000

Brad returned to the closet about five minutes later. The Carr brothers had had enough fun for now. It was time to get some money. Brad was the first chosen by the gunman to go to the bank's ATM drive-up. He was so nervous that he couldn't locate his keys. They then searched for HG's keys without success. "Somebody better find the fucking keys," one of the Carr brothers screamed, "I'm going to pop somebody's ass. Find the keys."[40] Finally, it was decided to use Jason's silver Dodge Dakota pickup truck, the keys for which were on top of the entertainment center in his room. Jonathan Carr remained at home with the captives while Reginald accompanied Brad to the Commerce Bank, where he withdrew $350 from his checking account and another $350 from his savings at 11:54 and 11:55 respectively. He attempted to extract more a minute later, but the transaction was denied.

While Brad and Reginald were driving to various banks, Jonathan decided to enjoy himself with the girls. He ordered HG out of the closet and escorted her just outside the bedroom into the hall-

The victims were driven to area ATMs where they were forced at gunpoint to withdraw and hand over their money.

way between the bedroom door and the wet bar. From that vantage point, he could still keep an eye on the closed closet door. "Get down on all fours and get yourself wet,"[41] he instructed her. HG got down and began

45

to masturbate to provide some lubrication for the sexual assault she anticipated. She didn't protest. She didn't break down. She resolved that she would do whatever needed to be done to make it through this ordeal. She slowly slid her middle finger in and out of her vagina. Jonathan placed the gun on the floor and unzipped his pants. HG looked down between her legs and saw the handgun lying there on the ground right between her two feet, only about twenty-four inches away. She thought quickly about grabbing it but was afraid she wouldn't be fast enough to seize it before her captor did. The whole quandary became moot when Jonathan grabbed her by the midriff and penetrated her from behind inserting his penis into her vagina. When he finished with her, Jonathan ordered her back into the closet.

Brad and Reginald, meanwhile, were en-route to the Prairie State Bank, where Brad withdrew a total of $1,150.00 in three separate transactions from 11:58 to 11:59. Finally, they drove to the ATM of the Central Bank and Trust where Brad made a couple of attempts to withdraw as little as $200.00 and then $100.00, but both transactions were denied. They returned to Birchwood Drive at about 12:15 A.M. and the Carr brothers were already $1,850 richer.

Reginald walked behind Brad as they entered the house and went back into Jason's room. Brad was immediately ordered to the closet and Reginald pulled Jason out. The two of them walked out to the pickup truck with Jason getting behind the wheel. He backed the truck out of the driveway, and drove to the Prairie State Bank ATM. It was 12:30 Friday morning when Jason withdrew the first $200.00 from his account. He tried twice more to withdraw an additional $200.00 and then twice to withdraw $100.00. None of those transactions were approved. Finally, at 12:34 A.M., Jason was able to extract $80.00 from his Capitol Federal account at the Commerce Bank ATM across the street from the Prairie State Bank. Irritated, Reginald instructed Jason to return to his house. The entire trip was much quicker than Brad's had been and by 12:40 in the morning Jason was returned to the closet.

"Who's next,"[42] Reginald barked. HG stood up to get ready to go, but Aaron said, "No, I'll go."[43] HG simply ignored him and proceeded to exit the closet. She grabbed her purse containing her ATM card and a white sweatshirt, which she pulled over her head in mid-stride while on her way out of the room. She and Reginald walked out the front door and onto the well-lit porch, then proceeded to Jason's truck. Reginald waved his gun toward the driver's door indicating for HG to get behind the wheel. He jumped into the truck and immediately crouched back into the passenger seat. HG carefully backed the truck out of the driveway.

Despite her caution, the truck slid on the ice-slicked driveway and into the road. HG turned the vehicle towards 127th Street and headed east to 21st Street, where she turned left heading in a westerly direction. "Don't look at me," Reginald told her as she turned her head to see if there were any oncoming cars prior to turning onto 21st street. She quickly turned away.

"What did my brother do to you,"[44] Reginald asked. "He forced me to have sex with him,"[45] HG responded. She was determined to tell her captor what he wanted to hear thinking it might appease him. Reginald laughed and said, "Did you like it?"[46] "Yes,"[47] HG answered almost choking over the word. He continued to probe. "Have you ever been with a black man before?"[48] "No,"[49] she said. "Was it better than your boy?"[50] "Yes,"[51] she retorted again almost gagging at the thought of it. "Baby, that's all right, you ain't got to lie to me,"[52] Reginald said. HG was silent.

Somewhere along the way, HG gathered up the courage to try to peer into the future. "Are you going to shoot us,"[53] she asked. "No,"[54] he answered. "You know, you can have whatever you want. Please don't hurt us,"[55] she begged. "Do you promise you're not going to shoot us or kill us?"[56] she asked as if trying to build a sense of rapport with him. "Yeah,"[57] he answered, as HG pulled the truck into the parking lot of the Commerce Bank. It was a bank with which HG was unfamiliar, but she found the drive-up ATM on north side of the lot and proceeded to drive to it. She rolled the window of the truck about two thirds the way down, retrieved the checkbook containing the ATM card from her purse, leaned out the window and inserted the card into the ATM. She entered her code and a request to withdraw $350.00. As she leaned out the window, Reginald reached over and rubbed his gloved hand on her vagina causing HG to fall forward onto the partially open window.

It was 12:53 A.M. when HG immediately tried to take another $200.00, but that transaction was denied. A third attempt yielded a withdrawal of $150.00. Once she had all the cash in hand, she turned and handed it to her assailant. "Do you want me to try again?"[58] HG asked him. "Is that all you got?[59] he responded. "Yeah,"[60] she answered, and was instructed to begin the short drive back to the house.

HG pulled the truck back into the driveway and exited the vehicle "I wish we could have met under different circumstances. I think you're cute. We probably could have hit it off,"[61] Reginald flirted as they walked to the front door. "Yeah, me too,"[62] HG answered a bit sarcastically. "What the fuck does that mean?"[63] he inquired rather abruptly. "Well, I'm not really having a good time,"[64] she said honestly.

As they entered the house, Reginald yelled out, "it's me."[65] Jonathan walked from behind the wall where he hid himself until he was sure it was his brother who was entering the condo. HG made her way back to the closet, noticing out of the corner of her eye that Heather was sitting on the floor by the wet bar. She didn't make eye contact and no words were spoken between them, but HG could detect that Heather was kind of spaced out as if in shock. HG continued directly back into the closet, getting in, as Aaron was taken out. It was about 1:10 A.M. when he and Reginald departed the house to go to the ATM at the Central Bank & Trust. Aaron was able to retrieve only $350.00, which he withdrew at 1:17 A.M. A second attempt at the same ATM was unsuccessful.

While Reginald and Aaron were away, Jonathan returned to the bar area and, looking at the bottle of liquor on the bar, asked Heather what *Weller's* was. "It's whiskey,"[66] she responded. He poured a drink, walked over to the closet, opened the doors, and held it out. "Anybody want a drink?"[67] he asked. There were no takers. He shut the closet doors again. Looking down, Jonathan discovered a big milk jug full of coins just outside the closet door. He picked it up, and that's when he noticed it. The popcorn tin that HG's mom had given Jason sat right next to his bed. He opened it and walked out to the bar. Holding up a diamond engagement ring he asked, "Whose is this?"[68] "It's probably HG's, but I don't know,"[69] Heather responded. "Which one is HG's,"[70] Jonathan asked, meaning which among the three men held captive was HG's boyfriend. "Jason,"[71] Heather answered. Jonathan walked back to the closet, opened the door, pointed the gun at Jason's head while holding the ring in front of him. "Is this the only one?[72] he asked hoping that there might be other gems in the house. "It's the only one,"[73] Jason said as he turned to look at HG, his heart almost breaking. Brad also looked at her. HG peered at Jason and noticed the red marks on his back. They were square shaped–three of them in all. She recognized the marks as the type that might be left from being struck on the back with a golf club and believed that it might have happened while she was at the ATM.

Between 1:30 A.M and 2:15 A.M

Aaron walked back into the closet joining Brad, Jason and HG. Heather was still out by the wet bar. Shortly after Aaron's arrival, Reginald called for "Shorty,"[74] a nickname he had given to HG, to come out of the closet. He escorted her to the dining room. HG noticed that the bathroom door was now closed, and Heather was no longer sitting by the bar. Reginald led HG to a place in the dining room generally occupied by the table, though it had been moved and was replaced by some empty boxes that once held the Christmas decorations. As they maneuvered through the dining area, Reginald asked about the earrings that HG wore. "They're fake,"[75] she said, "You know, you can have them if you want them."[76] As she started to remove them Reginald said, "No, I don't want them."[77] She laid them down on one of the Christmas boxes. Then, moving the gun into her back, he said, "Get down on all fours."[78] HG jerked forward in surprise at the sensation of a gun being pressed against her back. "Relax," he said. "I ain't gonna shoot you yet."[79] She began to panic. "Before," she thought to herself as she got down on her hands and knees, "he said he wasn't going to shoot me. Now he said he isn't going to shoot me *yet*."[80] Rather quickly, before she could analyze his comment any further, Reginald had penetrated HG's vagina with his penis. Reginald pulled back rather quickly and thrust forward with great force. It was quite painful for HG who was not well lubricated. The motion was tearing at the sensitive walls of her vagina. Within just a minute or two he told her to turn around and swallow it. She turned. Placing his penis in her mouth, Reginald ejaculated. HG swallowed hard.

Reginald then led her to the small bathroom and told her to open the door. HG saw Heather down on all fours being raped vaginally from behind. "Hold on, I'm not done,"[81] Jonathan said from inside, as he pushed the door closed with one hand. The two waited in the hall outside the door for a few minutes before Reginald instructed HG to open the door and go in. There was only about three feet between the sink and the door, making the room very tight for three people. It didn't seem to matter to Jonathan, who had already withdrawn his penis from Heather and readied himself for entry into HG's cut and swollen vagina. He instructed a compliant HG to get down on all fours. Once she was in position, he raped her, as Heather sat motionless and silently on the floor beside them. When he had completed his assault, Jonathan removed his condom and flushed it down the toilet.

Both girls were led from the bathroom and ordered to sit together on the floor near the bar. As they did so, "the intruders used cleaning solution to wipe various surfaces and objects in the house."[82]

A short time later, the girls were escorted out to the garage by one of the gunmen, while the other retrieved the three men from the closet and followed behind. The two girls were told to get into the trunk of Aaron's car. The men were given the same command. It was obvious, however, that five adults were not going to fit into the tiny trunk space of the Honda Accord. The brothers instituted a hastily devised "Plan B". The girls were taken out of the trunk and put into the back seat of Aaron's car, and the three men were told to get into the trunk. The trunk was closed, prompting Heather to ask HG how long she thought the guys might last in the closed trunk.

The Carr brothers opened the garage door and talked for a little bit. Heather was told to stay in the front passenger seat of the Accord while Reginald walked HG out of the garage toward Jason's truck that was parked in the driveway. As they walked, Jonathan said to Reginald, "if she gives you any trouble...let me know and we'll take care of that."[83] HG took a seat in the front passenger side of the pickup. The hostages were completely naked, except for the two women, who wore only sweaters. The brothers backed the vehicles onto Birchwood Drive and continued down 127th Street. "Where are we going," HG asked Reginald. He told her that he just wanted to drop them off far away from any of the cars. He continued driving to 21st Street then up Greenwich Avenue, under Highway 96 and onto a secluded stretch of road with a median down the middle. The area was unfamiliar to HG, who observed no houses in the vicinity. The dashboard digital clock read 2:07 A.M. All five hostages were taken out of the vehicles, ordered to kneel in the snow, and shot at close range in the back of their heads, execution style.

The snow-covered, partially constructed, barren soccer field at the end of this road was the place where the latest round of the Carr brother's victims would die, all except for one courageous elementary school teacher. As HG lay in the snow, she knew she had the ability to live, or die in the field. She promised herself at that moment that she would not die on this night. Rather, she would live.

Chapter 5
The Aftermath

Friday, December 15, 2000
Approximately 2:18 A.M to 2:45 A.M.

After leaving their victims for dead and disposing of the murder weapon, the Carr brothers returned to the condominium at 12727 Birchwood Drive. They needed to retrieve the tan Toyota, but also planned to quickly steal anything of value that remained in the condo before heading to their respective domiciles. Entering the house, one of the brothers went downstairs and grabbed the large television while the other went into Jason's bedroom to seize the jar of coins and the popcorn tin that contained the diamond ring. That's where he encountered Nikki, HG's little schnauzer. The dog barked and nipped at the intruder's ankles. It quickly became an annoyance to the burglar, who grabbed the golf club used to beat Jason and Aaron and slammed it down hard on the dog's neck. The blow caused a severe injury, almost separating the dog's head from the spinal cord and vertebrae. He then grabbed some sharp, pointy object that was within reach and stabbed the dog in the neck, leaving it dead on the floor.

After taking what they could, the two cold-blooded murdering thieves headed home.

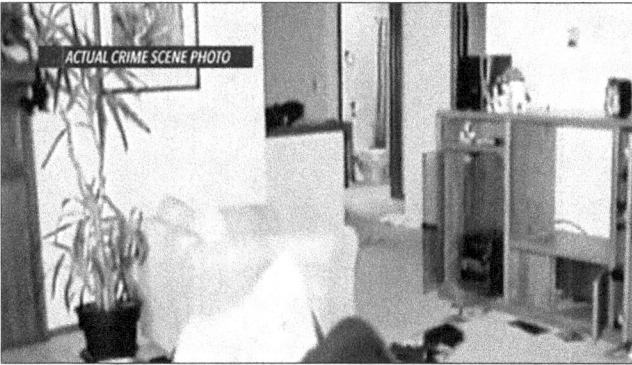

This is the way police found the house after it was ransacked by the murdering duo in their haste to steal whatever they considered to be of value.

The Investigation
Approximately 2:45 A.M

The 911 dispatcher had already alerted police to the major details of HG's call and separate units were responding to the Johnson home, where HG waited, the victims' home, and the soccer field. Deputy Sheriff Matthew Lynch of the Sedgwick County Police

Department was the first to arrive at the execution site. He immediately observed a lone Honda sitting to his west. He exited his vehicle and tactically approached the Honda.

The entrance to the soccer field (top) and the Honda (bottom) as Deputy Sheriff Lynch found them.

Dispatch had broadcast that the possible homicide suspects were at the intersection of 37th and Greenwich, so Lynch had no way of knowing if they were still in the area. He did know, however, that no one else would be checking in on this call. He was alone and not about to take any foolish chances. As he edged closer to the Honda, he began to notice the bodies, thinking to himself that it looked like something out of a movie set. He first saw two male bodies lying in the snow with a third body laying across them. Lying to the left of the male bodies was a fourth body, this one female. Then there was a gap with a blood spot in the snow signaling that someone was missing.

Lynch sprang into action. Bending down to the victims, he started to check their vitals. He could detect a pulse in neither Jason nor Heather although it appeared to him that both Aaron and Brad were attempting to breathe. Lynch used his radio to advise dispatch that there were four "code blue"[84] victims at the scene, implying that each was at least in cardiac arrest. Immediately, every available unit responded. Crime Scene Investigator Kevin Brasser was next to arrive at the soccer field. He immediately began to locate and photograph evidence. A few minutes later, at 12:54 A.M., EMS arrived on the scene and further examined the victims while police officers continued to comb the area for additional evidence. Investigators were able to locate on the snow-covered soccer field "spent

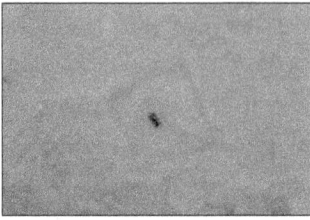

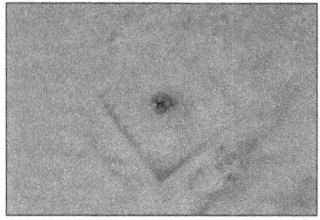

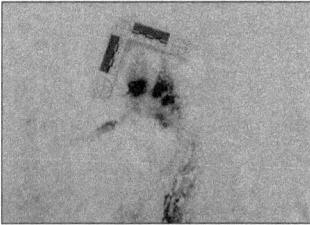

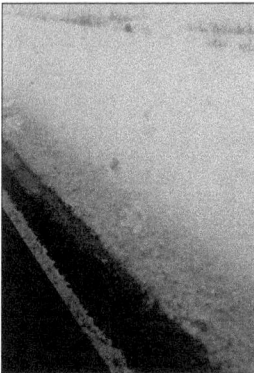

The variety of evidence was collected and/or photographed at the crime scene by investigators. These included (top row) a bullet fragment and a hair clip fragment, (second row) a glove and a footprint (bottom row) footprints leading to the road.

cartridge casings, bullet fragments, an ATM receipt reflecting a withdrawal at 1:17 that morning, and pieces of HG's plastic hair clip."[85]

Police and emergency medical support, meanwhile, arrived at the Johnson home, where HG once again relayed the horrific details of the recent events to police.

She was checked and treated by medical personnel, then transported to a local hospital emergency room with what appeared to be non-life-threatening injuries. HG had suffered a gunshot wound to the back of her head. The impact fractured her skull; but, in a miraculous turn of events, the bullet did not penetrate into her brain, apparently because it had been deflected by the plastic hair clip she was wearing. She also had bruises on her face, frostbite on her feet, multiple lacerations to her body, and several injuries resulting from the repeated sexual assaults.

The extent of HG's injuries, exposure to the icy temperatures of the brutal mid-December Kansas weather, and the physical and mental torture she had endured over the course of the four preceding hours, made HG's survival efforts even more heroic. Despite the personal trauma and the loss of four friends, HG's focus was not on the extent of her own injuries, but rather on the capture of the offending brothers. She showed extraordinary courage in the face of her horrific ordeal and, according to several police officers dispatched to the various crime scenes, hers is the single most heroic story of which they had ever heard.

With HG's vivid recall of the events, the investigation into the ghastly happenings of December 14 and 15, as well as the hunt for the perpetrators, were now underway.

3:00 A.M. – 3:59 A.M.

Wichita Police Officer Michael Dean had already arrived at the crime scene at 12727 Birchwood Drive. He was expecting to be joined at the house by Sergeant John Hoofer, but as Hoofer was on his way, a Dodge Dakota pickup truck matching the description of the vehicle that had been put out over the police radio, passed him heading in the opposite direction. Hoofer turned his vehicle around and began his pursuit. Unfortunately, the Sergeant lost sight of the truck, and turned his cruiser around to head back toward Birchwood Drive. He arrived at 3:19 A.M and met Officer Dean, who had waited for the Sergeant to arrive before entering the house.

ACTUAL CRIME SCENE FOOTAGE

The 12727 Birchwood Drive home of Sander, Befort and Heyka.

They did not expect to see what they found. The home had been ransacked. Drawers were dislodged from the bedroom dressers. Clothes were strewn about

and the beds were stripped of their linens. The entertainment center in the living room "had an open space
where a television would have been, and a coaxial cable
had been pulled through the open space and was lying
on the floor."[86] The lower level had also been ransacked. There was a computer desk with no computer
on it and "there was a large pool of blood on the corner
of the mattress and what appeared to be a bullet hole."[87]
The police also discovered the body of a dead dog. The
officers departed the house and properly secured it as a
crime scene.

While the evening's sole survivor was being treated
at the hospital, Jonathan Carr was planning his alibi, not
to the police, as it is doubtful the notion of being caught
ever crossed his mind, but rather to his girlfriend
Tronda Adams. At 3:31 A.M, Jonathan phoned her indicating that he missed a 2:30 A.M. train he had hoped
to take to Cleveland, Ohio. He asked if he could spend
the night at her place, and Tronda, though sharing the
home with her mother, obliged without hesitation. He
arrived at Tronda's home at 3:45 A.M. still wearing the
same cloths he donned during the attacks–the same
clothes in fact, that he wore when he and Reginald departed Adams' house in search of a victim at 9:30 P.M.
on December 14.

"Can you change a $20.00 bill for some ones?"[88]
Carr asked Tronda, pulling a wad of cash totaling at

least $500.00 from his pocket. "Where did you get all that money?"[89] she asked incredulously. She had never seen Jonathan with so much cash before. "I took all my money from the bank before leaving town,"[90] he responded. Tronda thought his explanation odd, knowing that he been unemployed and was from Dodge City, not Wichita. She really didn't give it much thought beyond that, however.

4:00 A.M.

Officer Dean was still standing by his patrol car in front of the 12727 Birchwood Drive residence when he observed a 1988 Plymouth driving toward the crime scene. He took note of the vehicle immediately, especially because there was no other traffic in this otherwise quiet and secluded neighborhood. Typically, there might be an isolated car or two traveling these roads at 4:00 in the morning, but with the slick, snow-covered street conditions that existed, he found the presence of a vehicle even more unusual. He paid particular attention as the vehicle rolled past him taking note of everything he could. The driver was a black male wearing a stocking cap. He stared straight ahead as he passed by Dean. He made no eye contact and didn't acknowledge the officer in any way. Nor did he bother to turn his head to gawk at the crime scene, something that very rarely–if ever–happens. If not for a heightened sense of awareness, Dean may have thought the man simply suffered from an amazing lack of curiosity, but there were other things that caught the officer's attention as he made a mental note of the Ford County license plate number. As the driver completed a U-turn heading onto 127th Street and back in the direction from which it came, Dean notified Sergeant Hoofer that he needed to make a traffic stop so as to identify the driver.

4:13 A.M. to 4:29 A.M.

Hoofer pulled the white Plymouth over at 4:15 A.M. as it was driving on 127th Street away from the area of the crime scene. He asked the driver for his license and registration, but his attention focused on the black leather coat that was laying across the car's rear seat. "Where are you heading," Hoofer inquired. "Stefanie Donley's apartment. She's my girlfriend," the driver answered, as he handed the officer the requested information. The license indicated that the man was Reginald Carr from Dodge City. From the description Reginald offered of Donley's apartment complex, however, Hoofer recognized its location as the 5400 block of East 21st Street–the Windsor at Woodgate apartments. Hoofer made some small talk and handed the license and registration back to Carr, who drove away immediately.

Jonathan, meanwhile, was still cultivating his plans. At 4:25 A.M. he made a phone call to Dodge City and at 4:26, he phoned his sister, waking her from a deep slumber. He told her that Reginald was coming over to trade cars with her.

At about the same time that Jonathan was formulating his shallow plan to cover up his crimes, the press was gathering at the home of Sander, Heyka and Befort.

Every major television outlet arrived at the crime scene and reported the details as they were received.

Rumors of the horrendous acts perpetrated by the Carr brothers were beginning to leak, and it wasn't long before virtually every news station arrived at the crime scene. Investigative Reporter Kris Cobel noted that every station was going live from the scene and disseminating information as they received it because everyone in the press knew that the two suspects were still running free, armed and extremely dangerous. All three major news stations reported on the pickup truck, the stolen television and engagement ring, and every other relevant and known detail of the gruesome events.

The news was being reported in real time and the coverage was wall-to-wall because it was a developing situation. As people awoke on the morning of Friday, December 15, they were inundated with reports of the vicious home invasion, assaults, and murders.

The Arrest of Reginald Carr
Approximately 4:30 A.M. to 7:30 A.M.

Reginald Carr arrived at his girlfriend's apartment. He stayed only about fifteen minutes before driving off, but returned again at 5:30 A.M. It was just about at that time that another resident of the Woodgate complex, Christian Taylor, turned on the local news as he prepared for work. He took note of the report of the murders, which indicated that the gunmen escaped in a silver Dodge Dakota pickup truck.

The Woodgate Apartment Complex

Taylor left his apartment at just about 6:25 A.M., making his way to his own vehicle. As he did so, he noticed that there was a Dodge Dakota pickup truck fitting the description of the one mentioned on the news, parked on the other side of the empty space next to his car. The tailgate of the pickup truck was down, and a large TV was sitting in its bed. A black man, later identified as Reginald Carr, emerged from behind the truck. He appeared to be in his 20s or 30s, had facial hair representing a few days' growth, and he wore blue jeans and a dark leather jacket. A scarf or hood covered his head. Taylor grew suspicious. He got in his car and headed to the nearby police station to report what he had seen.

Jason Befort's 1999 silver Dodge Dakota stolen by the Carr brothers and used to transport the stolen property from their victims' home to the Woodgate Complex apartment of Reginald's girlfriend.

At about the same time, Riwa Obel Nsangalufu, another resident at the complex, walked out of the building to warm up his car. As he did so, he saw Reginald Carr, a man he did not recognize, dragging a large television on a blanket toward building number 8. He, too, spotted the Dodge Dakota with its tailgate down. Reginald asked Nsangalufu if he could help carry the TV into the apartment he had just rented. Nsangalufu initially declined but eventually agreed, and the two men carried the large screen TV up a set of stairs and into apartment 819. Carr indicated that he could get it into the apartment himself and offered to pay Nsangalufu for his help. Reginald pulled a wad of folded bills from his pocket, but Riwa refused the money. Before Nsangalufu had departed the hallway, Carr knocked on the apartment door and Donley opened it, asking where he had been all night noting that she had been waiting for him. Carr made up a lie about his brother Jonathan seeing a married woman. When her husband caught them in the act, Reginald continued, the man began shooting at Jonathan, causing him to run off.

Reginald also said he had to clean some of his stuff out of his sister's garage and needed to bring them to Donley's apartment. At some point, Carr pulled about $900.00 out of his pocket, showing it to his girlfriend before undressing and heading into the shower. Donley noticed that Carr "removed a pair of red shorts, the

[same] ones he had been wearing under his pants the previous evening."[91]

While Nsangalufu was helping Carr carry the stolen television up the stairs to the second-floor hallway, a police officer investigating the report that Taylor had filed, discovered the Dodge pickup truck just as Taylor had described it. He followed the footprints and "drag marks" in the snow from the car to the sidewalk in front of the apartment complex where he found a discarded multicolored comforter. He also observed some clothing that had been thrown over the fence not far from the truck, and a blue-and-white-striped comforter in a trash dumpster next to the pickup truck. All these items were later identified as having been taken from the crime scene.

As the police officer was inspecting the grounds, Nsangalufu walked out of the apartment complex. The officer stopped him to ask some questions and Nsangalufu noted that he was on his way to work but had stopped "to help a man move a large TV from the truck to an apartment in building 8."[92] Upon request, Nsangalufu accompanied the officer to the hallway outside of apartment 819.

Jamie Crouch, one of the other police officers who responded to the Windsor at Woodgate apartments, took a position outside the balcony of apartment 819 while two other officers knocked on the apartment door announcing themselves as the police. Stephanie Donley, Reginald's "pretty, white, dark-haired girlfriend, opened the door."[93] Police officer Renay Bryand entered. "A few seconds later, the apartment's sliding glass door leading to the rear balcony opened. Reginald Carr emerged from the apartment; and placed his hands on a balcony railing as if he were going to jump from the balcony to the ground. Realizing that it was too high of a jump, and noticing police standing below, Carr returned to the apartment where Officer Bryand placed him under arrest at 7:30 A.M. On his person was Jason Befort's gas card, Heather Muller's watch, and $996.00 in cash, $980.00 of which was in crisp $20.00 bills, the type of which might be dispensed from an ATM.

The arrest of Reginald Carr

Police also discovered Brad Heyka's large-screen TV, wallet and watch, Jason Befort's checkbook, Aaron Sander's garment bag and computer, clothing, and jewelry. In addition they found HG's credit card.

During the course of the apartment search, the police retrieved Reginald Carr's leather coat, a glove and a stocking cap. The pocket of the coat contained ATM receipts showing early morning withdrawals from the account of Brad Heyka. The search of the pickup truck revealed more incriminating evidence, including Jason Befort's ATM card, wallet and driver's license, as well as several ATM receipts showing withdrawals from Jason's account at 12:31 and from HG's account at 12:53 that morning. The police were certain that they had a least one of the murderers.

As the sun began to rise, about ninety minutes prior to Carr's arrest, Wichita Police Lieutenant John Speer was at the crime scene at 12727 Birchwood Drive. A woman approached him and identified herself as Louis Muller, Heather Muller's mom. "My daughter never came home last night," she said. "Is she ok?" She asked the question already fearing the worse. "I'm sorry," were the only words Lt. Speer could manage to say. Mrs. Muller then asked if Aaron was ok. "No, he's not ok," Speer said. The veteran officer would later say of the exchange, "You're watching people's souls die right in front of you."

The Arrest of Jonathan Carr
Approximately 7:30 A.M. to 1:00 P.M.

Tronda Adams, meanwhile, was watching the morning news, when the report of the quadruple murder caught her attention. The newscaster said that "police were looking for two suspects, one wearing an orange FUBU shirt."[94] Alarmed, Adams awakened Jonathan with the news, eager to gauge his reaction. He showed no emotion indicating that he knew nothing of the murders. She questioned him further, noting that the report told of the gunmen taking the victims to ATMs, forcing them to withdraw cash. That seemed to get Jonathan's attention. "How do the police know that?"[95] he inquired. "One of the victims survived,"[96] she told him. Jonathan had to know that this wasn't good news for him.

Toni Greene had gone to her job as a home health care professional earlier in the morning but felt a bit queasy and left for home. Greene is Tronda's mother, but she was unaware that "Jonathan Carr had been courting her daughter for about a week."[97] By about 11:00 in the morning, she was feeling a bit better and started to clean the apartment. That's when she stumbled upon a maroon jewelry box containing a diamond engagement ring in one of the pockets of Jonathan's jacket. She logically assumed that it was intended for Jonathan's girlfriend in Ohio and immediately returned it to the coat pocket of the man who was sleeping on her couch.

At noon, Tondra took off her shoes and sat down to watch the news, hoping for an update on the quadruple murder. Jonathan, now awake, though still sprawled out on the couch, and Toni, were also in the living room. There on the screen was video coverage of Reginald Carr being arrested. Adams grew concerned and immediately told Jonathan to accompany her downstairs. "Did you just see that report," she inquired of him. "I did," he responded rather pensively. In the face of additional questions from Tondra, Jonathan stuck to his original lie insisting that after missing his train, he was just hanging around drinking at his sister's house. Tondra was not buying it. "You were wearing the orange FUBU sweater and the police already have your brother," she said. Jonathan became visibly upset, and started to cry.

Several miles away, Andrew Schreiber, the first of the Carr brothers' kidnap and robbery victims, also tuned in to the noon report and saw a face that "was sickeningly familiar. Schreiber phoned police to say he thought Reginald was one of the men who robbed him."[98]

Tondra's mother was still upstairs watching the news, and while she didn't make the connection between Reginald and Jonathan, she learned from the report that a diamond engagement ring was one of the items stolen in the robbery and attacks. She also learned the police were looking for a white Plymouth, a car similar to the one she had seen parked outside the apartment earlier that morning. Looking outside, she observed the car in the same spot. She yelled for her still barefoot daughter to come upstairs where she whispered that she believed the police were looking for Jonathan and that they needed to leave immediately. She relayed to her daughter the story about the engagement ring in Jonathan's pocket and the presence of the white Plymouth parked outside. Tondra was convinced and started looking for her shoes. "You can leave without your shoes," her frantic mother urged. "Let's go!"[99]

The area outside of Toni Greene and Tronda Adams apartment where Jonathan Carr was captured and taken into custody.

Greene grabbed her niece, who had been staying with them, and together, the three women left the building and ran across the street to the apartment of neighbor

Dawnyieka Buggs, telling her to call the police. As Tondra looked back toward her apartment, she saw Jonathan standing at the front door with a confused look wondering why Tondra was across the way. He was still wearing the orange FUBU sweater. As the bewildered Carr stood in the doorway, police arrived. Carr quietly moved back into the apartment, removed the FUBU sweater, and slipped out of the front door, running toward an alley. Police immediately began pursuit and apprehended him at 12:33 P.M. "two blocks away from Greene's home, hiding between a house's storm door and front door."[100] Carr had lost one of his shoes in the chase. In his pocket was in excess of $1,000 in cash. Returning to Tondra's apartment, police discovered the orange FUBU sweater, leather gloves, a brown leather jacket containing the engagement ring Jason Befort intended for HG, and Jonathan's identification card. Several additional items were retrieved from Jonathan's car, including two clocks belonging to Brad Heyka.

Making an Evidentiary Case Against the Carr Brothers Approximately 1:01 P.M to 5:00 P.M.

As a matter of routine in the arrest process for capital crimes, warrants are issued for bodily specimens. In the arrest of Jonathan Carr, police certainly followed that protocol. While he was being transported to the hospital by a police officer and detective Kelly Otis,

Carr asked the detective about a quadruple homicide that took place in Wichita a week earlier at the hands of other criminals. "Those suspects were arrested and charged with capital murder,"[101] the detective said. Carr asked what that meant, and, when told that it was a crime to which the death penalty was applied, he asked how the death penalty was administered. The detective responded that a convicted criminal receives a lethal injection. "Do they feel anything from that?"[102] Jonathan inquired after a long pause. "We've never been able to ask anyone,"[103] Otis replied.

Once at the hospital, medical staff extracted hair, blood, and saliva samples from Carr, pursuant to the warrant for DNA evidence. Police hoped to match these samples to any DNA evidence that might be found at 12727 Birchwood Drive, at the soccer field, in the vehicles, and on the victims.

Approximately 6:30 P.M. to 8:00 P.M.

At 6:30 P.M., police were able to show HG two photo arrays. She was asked if she could "identify 'any of the people in the pictures as the intruders.'"[104] Pointing to a man in position number two of the first photo array, HG indicated that the man's features, including his eyes and his hair, betrayed him as one of the men who attacked her. That man to whom she had pointed was Reginald Carr. She incorrectly identified the second gunman, however, thinking the man in the number one position of the second photo array had the Buckwheat-hair style that she recalled on her other captor. Jonathan Carr, however, was in position number four of that array.

Arrest photos of
Jonathan Carr (L) and Reginald Carr (R)

A bit later in the evening about–7:15 P.M.–detectives investigating the crimes visited Ann Walenta, the Carr brothers first shooting victim, who was still hospitalized from the wounds inflicted in the December 11 attack. Police presented her with a photographic lineup card that included both Carr brothers. "The recovering woman picked out Reginald as the man who shot her. She pointed to another man who rang a bell of familiarity. He was not Jonathan but a man in prison at the time [of her assault]."[105]

The result of the witness identification presented a problem for the prosecutors. While all three eyewitnesses (Andrew Schreiber, Ann Walenta and HG) identified Reginald Carr as a perpetrator, none of the three were able to positively identify Jonathan Carr as a participant in the crimes. He could offer any number of excuses as to how he came to be in possession of the engagement ring and some of the other items that seemed incriminating, but without victim identification placing him at the scene at the time of the rapes, sexual assaults, robberies and murders, the police knew prosecutors would have a difficult time getting a conviction of Jonathan on any of those counts.

Despite the concerns, prosecutors charged both Reginald and Jonathan Carr with one hundred and three crimes, "including five counts of capital murder and multiple counts of rape and robbery. They were also charged with animal cruelty."[106] Each of the brothers had been charged with the same fifty counts for the crime spree that lasted nine days. Reginald Carr had been charged with an additional three counts for being a felon in possession of a firearm.

Evidence Collected in the Days and Years Following December 15, 2000
The Autopsies

The medical examiner in Kansas performed autopsies on the bodies of the four Carr shooting victims who had died as a result of their attacks. The reports would be used as evidence in the trial of the accused and to provide to law enforcement officers and the prosecution team answers to several outstanding questions that may help in their quest to prosecute the Carr brothers. The autopsy reports concluded:[107]

---

*"**Heather Muller** died of a contact gunshot wound to her head. Her body showed bruising on her lower extremities. Injuries to her genital area were consistent with the application of force, and injuries to her knees were consistent with being placed on her hands and knees for the purpose of sexual intercourse.*

***Aaron Sander** died of a contact gunshot wound to his head. He sustained blunt trauma injuries to his head and neck; and his legs showed bruises, red discoloration, and scrapes. Injuries on his forehead and head were consistent with being hit with a golf club and the gun associated with the murders.*

***Jason Befort** died of an intermediate-range gunshot wound to his head. In addition, his body showed blunt trauma injuries. An injury to his buttocks was consistent with being hit with a golf club.*

***Brad Heyka** died of an intermediate-range gunshot wound to his head. His face showed blunt trauma injuries. All of the gunshot wounds to the four Birchwood murder victims were consistent with their bodies being in a kneeling position with their heads down when the bullets entered their skulls.*

***HG's dog** sustained 'severe injury and fracturing of the neck, almost to the point where the head had fallen down off of the support of the spinal cord and vertebrae, consistent with being struck with a golf club. The dog also sustained a puncture wound to its neck."*

Paul F. Caranci

Finding the Murder Weapon
March 19, 2001

A Winfield Correctional Facility inmate was working a clean-up detail near the intersection of Kansas Highway 96 and Greenwich Road in Wichita when he noticed something peculiar in the grass. He walked closer and discovered a Lorcin .380 caliber handgun lying there. He immediately called for his supervisor. The gun was collected and passed up the chain of command. It was eventually sent for ballistics testing, the result of which "demonstrated that all of the bullets, casings, and fragments associated with the Schreiber, Walenta and Birchwood Drive incidents came from the Lorcin .380 handgun. This included a casing found at the scene where Schreiber was left by his abductors, bullets and casings from Walenta's Yukon, a bullet from Walenta's chest, casings and a bullet fragment found at 29th and Greenwich Road, and a bullet from the body of Aaron Sander. Tronda Adams identified the Lorcin .380 as the black handgun that Jonathan Carr had given her the evening of December 11, 2000 and that she had returned to him on December 12, 2000.

Chapter 6
The Trial

Monday, September 5, 2002 to Tuesday, November 5, 2002

While the City of Wichita, pundits, and news reporters wrangled with the typical political issues raised when a member of one race commits a heinous crime against someone of another race, prosecution and defense teams

Chief Deputy District Attorney
Kim Parker

prepared for trial. The highly anticipated Carr brothers' trial began on Monday, September 5, 2002 with Judge Paul Clark presiding. The prosecution team was comprised of Chief Deputy District Attorney Kim Parker, who assisted District Attorney Nola Foulston. Reginald Carr also had a pair of lawyers, including lead attorney Jay Greeno and his assistant Val Wachtel. Mark Manna and Ron Evans served as lawyers for brother Jonathan Carr. After a lengthy voir dire that eliminated four potential participants, a jury comprised of seven men and five women, ten of which were white and only two black, was impaneled.

Over the course of eight weeks, a total of ninety-seven witnesses testified, mostly for the prosecution, and some eight hundred and fifty pieces of evidence were admitted into the trial. The most captivating testimony was provided by HG, the sole survivor of the attacks of December 14 and 15, who recounted the rapes and execution-style murders in grisly detail.

In addition to HG's testimony, other crucial and spellbinding witnesses included Mary Dudley, the Sedgwick County coroner, who spoke about the wounds inflicted on each of the victims during the rapes, the attacks, and the shootings. She noted that both Brad Heyka and Jason Befort were shot from a slight distance, while Heather Muller and Aaron Sander were shot while the gun was pressed against their heads. She told jurors that all three men had bruises on their bodies and described how the golf club may have been used in the attack causing those wounds.

Some members of the amazing team of police officers who gathered the evidence needed to convict the Carr brothers on almost all counts. From top left Det. Jim Merrick, Lt. Tom Speer, CSI Kevin Brasser, all of the Wichita Police Dept. FBI Special Agent Michael Tabman and Detective Timothy Relph of the Wichita Police.

Trauma surgeon Scott Porter used an anatomical mannequin to demonstrate to the jury how and where

Ann Walenta was shot. During his graphic testimony, one of the jurors fainted, causing the doctor to step down from the witness stand to attend to the fifty-one-year-old juror.

Barbara Siwek, the Police Department Crime Scene Investigator, explained to the jury how the beating and death of HG's dog Nikki had come about and also provided evidence that the hair clip that HG wore on December 15 actually saved her life by deflecting the path of the bullet, causing it to only graze her head rather than penetrate her skull.

Andrew Schreiber also "took the stand and told the jury how he had been kidnapped, robbed, and then left in a field. He identified Reginald Carr as one of the two men who abducted him but could not identify Jonathan Carr."[108]

Even women who were considered friends of the Carr brothers testified against them. Tronda Adams implicated Jonathan in both the Schreiber kidnapping and the shootings on December 15. Tronda's mother Toni Greene explained how she discovered the diamond engagement ring in Jonathan's coat pocket. Stephanie Donley, Reginald's girlfriend, testified about the large amount of cash he carried despite not having a job and saying she lent him her Toyota Camry on the evening of December 14, and that he returned it twelve hours later. Donley's testimony also linked "Reginald to possessions stolen from the victims when she said he moved several items into her home, which were identified as belonging to [the victims]."[109]

Donley, a nurse by profession, also testified that she recognized a sexually transmitted disease, genital warts, on her boyfriend's private parts early in their relationship. A medical expert would later testify that HG had contracted genital warts.

Evidence presented in support of the prosecution's case included the gun discarded by the Carr brothers as they fled the soccer field, Jonathan Carr's recovered shoe which matched a shoe print left on a windshield sunshade found at the Birchwood Drive residence, DNA evidence that matched Jonathan's semen found both on a carpet at the residence and inside Heather Muller, and Heather's blood, which had spattered on Reginald Carr's clothing. Jonathan Carr's DNA was also found in samples from HG's rape examination. Semen collected from HG's labia majora matched Jonathan Carr's DNA and a sample of her vaginal discharge was consistent with DNA from her and Jonathan Carr, while all others at the Birchwood home were excluded as contributors. Jonathan's semen was also found on a swab of HG's lips. Despite the lack of an eyewitness identification, the prosecution made it very clear to the jury that Jonathan was not only at the scene of the crimes but was a very active participant in them.

Throughout the entire trial, the brothers' lack of remorse was evident in their behavior and mannerisms. Reginald Carr was seen smirking and smiling several times as witness after witness described the insidious nature of his crimes. More than once, the judge found it necessary to remove Reginald from the courtroom for his outrageous behavior, which included blowing kisses to those testifying against him.

The prosecution rested on October 25, 2002 and the defense presented its case. It was a pathetically weak defense. Jonathan's attorneys relied on the unused train ticket that he planned to use at the time of the quadruple homicides. The ticket was the only piece of evidence that the defense would introduce and only served to convince the jurors that Jonathan was in fact still in town at the time that the crimes were committed. Attempting to "emphasize the vagueness"[110] of HG's initial description of Reginald, his attorneys had the court replay the police interview that she provided on the night of the four murders. Giving the opportunity for the jurors to relive her gruesome and explicit statement, however, probably helped the prosecution at the expense of Reginald and Jonathan. Other than that, the two brothers simply blamed each other as their primary means of defense.

In the state's final summation, Kim Parker said, "This is a crime driven by greed and lust, by selfishness and driven by twisted sexual gratification."[111] For their part, the "defense attorneys for each Carr brother pointed fingers at the other. Wachtel emphasized there were inconsistencies in witness identification and noted DNA at the crime scene belonged to Jonathan rather than to Reginald. Mark Manna reminded the jury that both Ann Walenta and Andrew Schreiber had identified Reginald but not Jonathan. Reginald was the one found with most of the belongings stolen that night, Manna elaborated. 'Reginald was not alone, but the evidence will show who was playing the lead role that night – directing things, taking things...Don't just go back there and check the box guilty on all counts. Please consider [Jonathan's] guilt and innocence separate from damning evidence against his brother.'"[112]

On Tuesday, November 5, 2002, after deliberating for only fourteen hours, the jury returned with a verdict in the case of Wichita vs. Reginald and Jonathan Carr. The jury convicted Reginald on all fifty-three counts, while Jonathan was convicted on forty-three of his fifty counts. The brothers, shackled and standing with their attorneys when the verdict was read, exhibited no emotion. Families of the victims, however, "hugged one another as well as the prosecutors and a crime scene investigator who worked the case."[113] [Assistant District Attorney] Parker cried as she hugged HG. Parker told reporters, "Justice has been served and it is long awaited."[114] Noting the jury's reluctance to convict Jonathan Carr of the Schreiber crimes, Parker called them a "thinking person's jury"[115] because they felt that there was reasonable doubt as to whether Jonathan participated in those crimes.

Chapter 7
A Penalty That Fits the Crime

Tuesday, November 5, 2002

Despite the length of the trial and their thoughtful fourteen-hour verdict, the jury was not done. Rather, they were immediately charged with the awesome responsibility of determining what punishment to impose on the Carr brothers.

In this penalty phase of the case, the defense addressed the violent and abusive childhood the two brothers had experienced. The violence they witnessed growing up, the abandonment, beatings and deprivation they endured at the hands of those they trusted and loved. Forensic psychologist Mark Cunningham blamed their terrible childhood for their offenses, describing their upbringing as "combining the 'five Hs:

hopeless, helpless, homeless, hungry, and hug-less."[116] Under cross examination, however, even Cunningham was obliged to admit that, despite their horrible past, the Carr brothers still knew the difference between right and wrong. Speaking of Jonathan, Cunningham said, "There is no question he has awareness of his wrongful behavior."[117] "He doesn't care?"[118] Parker asked. "That's correct,"[119] the psychologist responded. Once again, the overall impact of a defense witness was more harmful to the Carr brothers than it was helpful.

Perhaps the biggest jury impact came, not from the mouths of witnesses, but rather from the mouths of the victims themselves. Andrew Schreiber said that because he still lives in Wichita, "There are constant reminders every day...One of the other effects this case has had on me are the feelings of [survivor's] guilt. I equate these feelings of guilt to ones that a soldier might go through."[120]

HG, with heartfelt eloquence, noted,

"I speak on behalf of Brad, Aaron, Heather, Ann, Andy, Jason and myself. One of my favorite 7-year-olds lost her uncle on the 15th.... This year, when her mom asked her what she wanted for Christmas, she replied that she had wings, and if they were real, that she could fly to heaven and she could see her Uncle Jason and her papa.... I wish life were that simple. I wish

that I could put on a pair of wings and that I could go see Jason—But we all know that these are wishes, and they are wishes that we have to wish because of two soulless monsters.... Every day there is a memory or a scar that reminds me of that night. I wake up in sweats from my nightmares. I pace at night because of noises that I think are somebody breaking into my house. And every morning, I carefully blow-dry my hair to cover up the spot that can no longer grow hair. I look at my knees and see the scars from the carpet burns that I got from the rape and in the back of [my] mind I wonder will it happen again."[121]

Her statement clearly touched the jurors.

The most touching statement, however, was that of Heather's mother Lois Muller. Noting that her heart breaks daily and that the heartbreak will last forever, she said,

Heather's eyes were filled with light and love and the spirit of God because she was filled with light and love and the spirit of God. When you look into Reginald and Jonathan Carr's eyes, they have a hollow, empty look, the look of pure evil and hatred, and I know this because I have looked into their eyes."

Noting the horrific things her daughter had to endure, Lois continued,

"My husband still looks in her bedroom every day thinking he is going to find her there. He misses her, and he carries this guilt that he wasn't there when she needed him. My mother can't get past December 15. Her every waking hour is spent dwelling on Heather's (being) dead in this crime. She's not the grandmother Heather knew and loved. She's no longer a functioning grandmother to her other grandchildren...I want to be able to hold Heather again and tell her goodnight, God bless you, I love you. I can only hold her picture and it's so flat and lifeless. I know Heather is in heaven, but I wasn't ready for it to be so soon."[122]

Ron Evans summed up on behalf of Jonathan by reminding the jurors of his client's background and lack of a serious criminal record prior to those nine days in December 2000. Reginald's attorney, Jay Greeno, simply asked the jury for mercy for Reginald, the "mercy that he did not extend to those four individuals."[123] District Attorney Nola Foulston asked the jurors to let justice, not sympathy, be their goal in establishing the penalty to be imposed. "You can't blame your family for what went wrong in your life,"[124] she said to the jury. "We know from the evidence they committed these crimes because they wanted to, because they chose to,"[125] she said.

Friday, November 15, 2002

Despite the expert testimony of two forensic psychologists, a medical doctor, and a peer reviewer of the Journal of Nuclear Medicine, Reginald's estranged wife and mother of his child, the mother of another of Reginald's children, a woman who had once hired Jonathan to do some handywork, and a very emotional plea from the Carrs' own mother, it took the jury only seven hours to recommend that both Reginald and Jonathan Carr be put to death by lethal injection, a penalty many in Kansas thought appropriate. "For each defendant, the jury returned four death sentences for the murders of Aaron Sander, Brad Heyka, Jason Befort and Heather Muller, a life sentence for Walenta's murder, and over forty years of consecutive imprisonment for the remaining convictions."[126]

Conclusion

March 2004

The jury was long ago dismissed, with the gratitude of the court and an appreciative public. The Carr brothers' saga, however, was far from over. In March 2004, the courts ruled on a wrongful death lawsuit against the state of Kansas brought by the families of the victims just six months earlier. In October 2004, the Associated Press reported that three of the families were to share $1.7 million or almost $567,000 each, while the fourth family would receive $450,000.

December 2005

Twenty-one months later, the Kansas Supreme Court overturned the Carr brothers' death penalty saying, in part, that the presiding trial judge, the late Paul Clark, erred when refusing to separate both the trial and the penalty phase of Reginald and Jonathan Carr.* The Kansas Supreme Court's verdict sparked outrage in the community, rekindling talk of "reverse racism." The

---

* *The Kansas Supreme Court reversed the death sentences; the court ruled that the juries should have been affirmatively instructed that mitigating circumstances need not be proved beyond a reasonable doubt. Additionally, the Kansas Supreme Court ruled that the Carrs should have been tried separately. The Kansas attorney general filed an appeal to the United States Supreme Court, which granted certiorari to review the Kansas Supreme Court's rulings.*

case was appealed all the way to the United States Supreme Court, which granted the writ of certiorari.

Wednesday, October 7, 2015 to Wednesday, January 20, 2016

The case was argued before the US Supreme Court on October 7, 2015 in an unusually long hearing that lasted some two hours. Subsequently, the court rendered an 8-1 decision on January 20, 2016. "Writing for the majority, Justice Antonin Scalia held that the Eighth Amendment to the United States Constitution does not require courts in capital cases to instruct juries about the burden of proof for establishing mitigating evidence; therefore, the trial courts in this case were under no obligation to inform

The United States Supreme Court heard oral arguments in the case of Reginald and Jonathan Carr and overturned the decision by the Kansas Supreme Court to throw out the death sentences.

jurors that 'mitigating circumstances *need not* be proved beyond a reasonable doubt'.

Because the jury instructions in this case told jurors to 'consider *any* mitigating factor', Justice Scalia concluded that '[j]urors would not have misunderstood these instructions to prevent their consideration of constitutionally relevant evidence.' Justice Scalia also concluded that in light of the evidence presented at trial, the joint trial of defendants 'did not render the sentencing proceedings fundamentally unfair.' Justice Scalia then ordered the case remanded back to the Kansas state court for reconsideration."[127]

In a dissenting opinion, Justice Sonia Sotomayor "argued that the Supreme Court should not have reviewed these cases because Kansas did not violate any party's constitutional rights. She also expressed concern that the majority's opinion would discourage states from developing techniques for ensuring fair procedures during capital trials."[128]

With the United States Supreme Court's reversal of the decision by the Kansas Supreme Court, the death penalties imposed on Reginald and Jonathan Carr were reinstated. The two brothers currently sit on death row at the El Dorado Correctional Facility in Kansas.

A Silver Lining

For Andrew Schreiber and HG, the sole survivors of the Carr brothers' December reign of terror, life would never be the same. The two, suffering from the post-traumatic stress of such horrific events, and the fear and trepidation that such stress carries, may understandably never forget the ordeal each was forced to endure in December 2000. Yet, despite the loss of trust in people, the hesitance to walk alone at night, or entertain even the well-intentioned plea of a stranger, there is some happiness that each experienced as a result.

During the trial of Reginald and Jonathan Carr, HG and Andrew became acquainted. They also became friends and shortly thereafter, they began to date. On October 2, 2004, HG became Andrew Schreiber's wife in a quiet ceremony in Kansas. The couple moved about 170 miles northeast of Wichita but continue to call Kansas home. According to family friend Stephanie Carlson, the couple now has two children and live hap-pily. They relocated to the small City of Shawnee, Kan-sas where HG teaches fourth grade at the Mize Elemen-tary School.

In March 2010, minutes before HG was to start her school day, the Mize principal called an emergency meeting. HG didn't think such an impromptu meeting so close to the start of school could bring good news. She could not have been more wrong, however, as school Superintendent Ron Wimmer, along with Principal Pam Hargrove, announced that HG had been named De Soto USD 232 Elementary Teacher of the Year."[129] The award is given each year in recognition of excellence in the classroom and HG was chosen as the 2010 district honoree.

In accepting the distinction, a humble HG told reporters and fellow educators that she was honored to be recognized in such a way. "Children have an innocence about them that is not found anywhere else," HG said. "It's nice to be able to come to work and to have their view of the world surround me instead of the cynical view that most adults have."[130]

Understanding the horrific adult experiences that HG was forced to endure, it is hard to disagree with her.

Notes

[1] The Eighteenth Judicial District District Court, Sedgwick County, Kansas Criminal Department. Transcript of Preliminary Hearing April 16, 2001. The Testimony of HG. in response to questions by Sedgwick County District Attorney, Nola Foulston.

[2] Ibid.

[3] Ibid.

[4] Ibid.

[5] Ibid.

[6] The United States Supreme Court Writ of Certiorari in the Case of State of Kansas v Reginald Dexter Carr, Jr., October 2014. Appendix Page 29.

[7] Ibid.

[8] Ibid.

[9] Ibid.

[10] Ibid. Appendix Page 30.

[11] Ibid.

[12] Ibid. Appendix Page 31.

[13] Ibid.

[14] Ibid. Appendix Page 32.

[15] Ibid.

[16] Noe, Denise, Crime Library: Criminal Minds & Methods. The Wichita Horror: Shattering Crimes. Chapter 1, page 1.

[17] The United States Supreme Court Writ of Certiorari in the Case of State of Kansas v Reginald Dexter Carr, Jr., October 2014. Appendix Page 33.

[18] Ibid.

[19] Ibid. Appendix Page 34.

[20] Ibid.

[21] Kieler, Ashlee, Mize Teacher Surprised by District's Honor, The Shawnee Dispatch, April 7, 2010. http://www.shawneedis-patch.com/news/2010/apr/07/mize-teacher-surprised-district-honor/. Page 1.

[22] Ibid.

[23] See interior and exterior images of the property at 12727 Birchwood Drive on Trulia - https://www.trulia.com/p/ks/wichita/12727-e-birchwood-dr-wichita-ks-67206--1079507543.

[24] The Eighteenth Judicial District District Court, Sedgwick County, Kansas Criminal Department. Transcript of Preliminary Hearing April 16, 2001. The Testimony of HG Glover in response to questions by Sedgwick County District Attorney, Nola Foulston.

[25] Ibid.

[26] Ibid.

[27] Ibid.

[28] Ibid.

[29] Ibid.

[30] Ibid.

[31] Ibid.

[32] The United States Supreme Court Writ of Certiorari in the Case of State of Kansas v Reginald Dexter Carr, Jr., October 2014. Appendix Page 37.

[33] Ibid.

[34] Ibid.

[35] The Eighteenth Judicial District District Court, Sedgwick County, Kansas Criminal Department. Transcript of Preliminary Hearing April 16, 2001. The Testimony of HG Glover in response to questions by Sedgwick County District Attorney, Nola Foulston.

[36] Ibid.

[37] Ibid.

[38] Ibid.

[39] Ibid.

[40] Ibid.

[41] Ibid.

[42] Ibid.

[43] Ibid.

[44] Ibid.

---

[45] Ibid.

[46] Ibid.

[47] Ibid.

[48] Ibid.

[49] Ibid.

[50] Ibid.

[51] Ibid.

[52] Ibid.

[53] Ibid.

[54] Ibid.

[55] Ibid.

[56] Ibid.

[57] Ibid.

[58] Ibid.

[59] Ibid.

[60] Ibid.

[61] The United States Supreme Court Writ of Certiorari in the Case of State of Kansas v Reginald Dexter Carr, Jr., October 2014. Appendix Page 40.

[62] Ibid.

[63] Ibid.

[64] Ibid.

[65] The Eighteenth Judicial District District Court, Sedgwick County, Kansas Criminal Department. Transcript of Preliminary Hearing April 16, 2001. The Testimony of HG Glover in response to questions by Sedgwick County District Attorney, Nola Foulston.

[66] Ibid.

[67] Ibid.

[68] Ibid.

[69] Ibid.

[70] Ibid.

[71] Ibid.

[72] Ibid.

[73] Ibid.

74 Ibid.

75 Ibid.

76 Ibid.

77 Ibid.

78 Ibid.

79 Ibid.

80 Ibid.

81 Ibid.

82 The United States Supreme Court Writ of Certiorari in the Case of State of Kansas v Reginald Dexter Carr, Jr., October 2014. Appendix Page 42.

83 The United States Supreme Court Writ of Certiorari in the Case of State of Kansas v Reginald Dexter Carr, Jr., October 2014. Appendix Page 43.

84 Supreme Court of Kansas, State of Kansas, Appellee, v Reginald Dexter Carr, Jr., Appellant. No. 90,044. Decided: July 25, 2014. The Police Officer's Report.

85 Ibid.

86 Ibid.

87 Ibid.

88 Ibid.

89 Ibid.

90 Ibid.

91 Ibid.

92 Ibid.

93 Noe, Denise, Crime Library: Criminal Minds & Methods. The Wichita Horror: Shattering Crimes. Chapter 4, page 8.

94 Supreme Court of Kansas, State of Kansas, Appellee, v Reginald Dexter Carr, Jr., Appellant. No. 90,044. Decided: July 25, 2014. The Police Officer's Report.

95 Ibid.

96 Ibid.

97 Noe, Denise, Crime Library: Criminal Minds & Methods. The Wichita Horror: Shattering Crimes. Chapter 4, page 8.

98 Ibid. Page 9.

[99] Ibid. Page 8.

[100] Ibid.

[101] Supreme Court of Kansas, State of Kansas, Appellee, v Reginald Dexter Carr, Jr., Appellant. No. 90,044. Decided: July 25, 2014. The Police Officer's Report.

[102] Noe, Denise, Crime Library: Criminal Minds & Methods. The Wichita Horror: Shattering Crimes. Chapter 4, page 9.

[103] Ibid.

[104] Supreme Court of Kansas, State of Kansas, Appellee, v Reginald Dexter Carr, Jr., Appellant. No. 90,044. Decided: July 25, 2014. The Police Officer's Report.

[105] Noe, Denise, Crime Library: Criminal Minds & Methods. The Wichita Horror: Shattering Crimes. Chapter 4, Page 8.

[106] Ibid. Chapter 6, Page 10.

[107] The United States Supreme Court Writ of Certiorari in the Case of State of Kansas v Reginald Dexter Carr, Jr., October 2014. Appendix Page 58.

[108] Noe, Denise, Crime Library: Criminal Minds & Methods. The Wichita Horror: Shattering Crimes. Chapter 4, Page 11.

[109] Ibid. Page 12.

[110] Ibid.

[111] Ibid.

[112] Ibid.

[113] LJ World.com, Lawrence Journal-World, "Carrs Found Guilty of Murder." November 5, 2002, https://www2.ljworld.com/news/2002/nov/05/carrs_found_guilty/.

[114] Ibid.

[115] Ibid.

[116] Noe, Denise, Crime Library: Criminal Minds & Methods. The Wichita Horror: Shattering Crimes. Chapter 4, Page 14.

[117] Ibid.

[118] Ibid.

[119] Ibid.

[120] Lassiter, The Wichita Eagle, "Victims' and Families of Victims' Statements in Court at Sentencing in the Wichita Massacre Trial," Saturday, November 16, 2002.

[121] Noe, Denise, Crime Library: Criminal Minds & Methods. The Wichita Horror: Shattering Crimes. Chapter 4, Pages 14 & 15.

[122] Lassiter, The Wichita Eagle, "Victims' and Families of Victims' Statements in Court at Sentencing in the Wichita Massacre Trial," Saturday, November 16, 2002.

[123] Noe, Denise, Crime Library: Criminal Minds & Methods. The Wichita Horror: Shattering Crimes. Chapter 4, Page 15.

[124] Ibid.

[125] LJ World.com, Lawrence Journal-World, "Carr Trial's Penalty Phase Begins, Defense Team Points to Dysfunctional Childhood in Effort to Spare Brothers' Lives," November 6, 2002, https://www2.ljworld.com/news/2002/nov/06/carr_trials_penalty/.

[126] Harvard Law Review, 130 Harv. L. Rev. 367, Capital Punishment, Kansas v. Carr, Leading Case: 136 S. Ct. 633 (2016), November 10, 2016. https://harvardlawreview.org/2016/11/kansas-v-carr/.

[127] Kansas v. Carr, Wikipedia, https://en.wikipedia.org/wiki/Kansas_v._Carr.

[128] Ibid.

[129] Kieler, Ashlee, Mize Teacher Surprised by District's Honor, The Shawnee Dispatch, April 7, 2010. http://www.shawneedispatch.com/news/2010/apr/07/mize-teacher-surprised-district-honor/.

[130] Ibid.

Bibliography

Blanco, Juan Ignacio, Murderpedia, "Reginald & Jonathan CARR," Noe, Denise, Crime Library: Criminal Minds & Methods, "The Wichita Horror," 2005.

Farias, Cristian, The Huffington Post, "Wichita Massacre' Brothers Get Zero Sympathy From the Supreme Court: Kansas Hasn't Executed Anyone in 50 Years. Will It Start Now?" January 20, 2016. https://www.huffpost.com/entry/wichita-massacre-supreme-court_n_569febcde4b076aadcc...

Harvard Law Review, 130 Harv. L. Rev. 367, Capital Punishment, Kansas v. Carr, Leading Case: 136 S. Ct. 633 (2016), November 10, 2016. https://harvardlawreview.org/2016/11/kansas-v-carr/.

Hegeman, Roxana, "Psychologist Details Carr's Troubled Childhood" [Wichita Massacre], AP/Topeka Capital-Journal, November 8, 2002. http://www.freerepublic.com/focus/news/785069/posts.

Kansas v. Carr, Wikipedia, https://en.wikipedia.org/wiki/Kansas_v._Carr.

Kieler, Ashlee, Mize Teacher Surprised by District's Honor, The Shawnee Dispatch, April 7, 2010.

http://www.shawneedispatch.com/news/2010/apr/07/
mize-teacher-surprised-district-honor/.

Lassiter, The Wichita Eagle, "Victims' and Families of
Victims' Statements in Court at Sentencing in the
Wichita Massacre Trial," Saturday, November 16,
2002.

LJ World.com, Lawrence Journal-World, "Wichita
Slayings Autopsies Shared," October 23, 2002,
https://www.2.ljworld.com/news/2002/oct/23/wich-
ita_slayings_autopsies/.

LJ World.com, Lawrence Journal-World, "Carrs Found
Guilty of Murder." November 5, 2002, https://www2.lj
world.com/news/2002/nov/05/carrs_found_guilty/.

LJ World.com, Lawrence Journal-World, "Carr Trial's
Penalty Phase Begins, Defense Team Points to Dysfunctional Childhood in Effort to Spare Brothers'
Lives," November 6, 2002, https://www2.ljworld.
com/news/2002/nov/06/carr_trials_penalty/.

Oxygen, Killer Siblings, 105 Carr Program Meter,
ID:XYKRS00105H. Scott Steinberg Productions. KS –
105 CAR, TVD #Q8505. https://vimeo.com/37581285,
Sedgwick County, Kansas Sheriff's Office, 141 West
Elm, Wichita, Kansas. Provider of some of the photo-
graphs used in this book.

Supreme Court of Kansas, State of Kansas, Appellee, v Reginald Dexter Carr, Jr., Appellant. No. 90,044. Decided: July 25, 2014. The Police Officer's Report.

Sylvester, Ron, "What Prosecutors Say Happened," The Wichita Eagle, October 2002

Sylvester, Ron, "Heather Muller's Life Was Filled With Music," The Wichita Eagle, October 4, 2002.

Sylvester, Ron, "Woman Testifies That Carrs Killed Her Friends in a Soccer Field," The Wichita Eagle, October 10, 2002.

Sylvester, Ron, "Trial Opens Window Into Night of Fear," The Wichita Eagle, October 13, 2002.

Sylvester, Ron, "Evidence in Carr Trial Gruesome, Unavoidable," The Wichita Eagle, October 23, 2002

Sylvester, Ron, "DNA Lets the Dead Speak in Carr Trial," The Wichita Eagle, October 27, 2002.

The Eighteenth Judicial District District Court, Sedgwick, County, Kansas Criminal Department Transcript of Preliminary Hearing April 16, 2001. The Testimony of HG.

The United States Supreme Court Writ of Certiorari in the Case of State of Kansas v Reginald Dexter Carr, Jr., October 2014.

The Washington Times, "Coroner Tells of Abuse Before Deaths," October 23, 2002.

Webster, Stephen, "The Wichita Massacre," American Renaissance, Front Page Magazine July 16, 2002.

Webster, Stephen, "The Wichita Massacre," American Renaissance, Vol. 13 No. 8, August 2002.

About the Author

Paul F. Caranci is a third-generation resident of North Providence and has been a student of history for many years. Paul served as Rhode Island's Deputy Secretary of State from 2007 to 2015 and was elected to the North Providence Town Council where he served from 1994 to 2010. He has a BA in political science from Providence College and is working toward an MPA from Roger Williams University.

Together with his wife Margie he founded the Municipal Heritage Group in 2009. He is an incorporating member of the Association of Rhode Island Authors (ARIA) and a member of the board of the RI Publications Society. He also served on the Board of Directors of the Heritage Harbor Museum and the Rhode Island Heritage Hall of Fame. He is past Chairman of the Diabetes Foundation of Rhode Island (formerly the American Diabetes Association, Rhode Island Affiliate) where he served on the Board for over 15 years.

During his tenure on the North Providence Town Council Paul's efforts earned him several awards. For his legislative work in the prevention of youth addiction to tobacco Paul was recognized with the James Carney Public Health Award from the RI Department of Health and an Advocacy Award from the American Cancer Society. Paul's legislation to expand health care coverage to include the equipment, supplies and education necessary for the home management of diabetes and his work toward the elimination of the pre-existing condition clause from health insurance policies written in Rhode Island were recognized with an Advocate of the Year Award from the Diabetes Foundation of RI and an Advocacy Award from the American Diabetes Association. Those new laws also made Rhode Island the first state in the nation to both eliminate the pre-existing condition clause and expand coverage for diabetes care. His efforts in exposing political corruption in his hometown earned him the Margaret Chase Smith Award for Political Courage from the National Association of Secretaries of State, the group's highest honor.

Paul is the author of ten published books including four award winning books. *The Hanging & Redemption of John Gordon: The True Story of Rhode Island's Last Execution* (The History Press, 2013) was voted one of the top five non-fiction books of 2013 by the Providence Journal. *Scoundrels: Defining Corruption Through Tales of Political Intrigue in Rhode Island* (Stillwater River Publications, 2016) was the winner of the 2016 Dorry Award as the non-fiction book of the year. *The Promise of Fatima: One Hundred Years of History, Mystery, and Faith* (Stillwater River

Publications, 2017) earned Paul a spot as a finalist in the International Book Awards, and *I Am The Immaculate Conception: The Story of Bernadette of Lourdes*, (Stillwater River Publications, 2019) landed Paul the same honor. Paul's memoir, *Wired: A Shocking True Story of Political Corruption and the FBI Informant Who Risked Everything to Expose It* (Stillwater River Publications, 2017) tells his own story of courage in the face of the political corruption that surrounded him.

Paul and his wife Margie recently celebrated their 42nd wedding anniversary. The couple have two adult children, Heather and Matthew; and four grandchildren, Matthew, Jacob, Vincent and Casey. They continue to make residence in the Town of North Providence.

Also By the Author

The History Press
2012

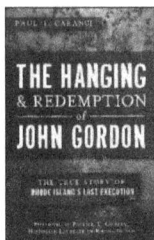

The History Press
2012
Named one of top 5
non-fiction books
of the year

Stillwater River Publications
2014

Stillwater River Publications
2014

Stillwater River Publications
2015

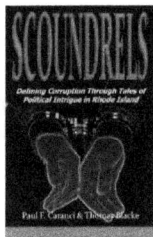

Stillwater River Publications
2016
Dorry Award
Non-fiction Book

Stillwater River Publications
2017

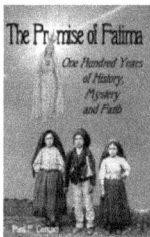

Stillwater River Publications
2017
Finalist in the 2018
International Book
Awards of the Year

Stillwater River Publications
2019
Finalist in the 2019
International Book Awards

Stillwater River Publications
2019

ORDER FORM

Please use the following to order additional copies of:

1. Heavenly Portrait: The Miraculous Image of Our Lady of Guadalupe **($20.00)**

2. I Am the Immaculate Conception: The Story of St. Bernadette And Her Apparitions At Lourdes **($20.00)**

3. The Promise of Fatima: One Hundred Years of History, Mystery & Faith **($20.00)**

4. Wired: A Shocking True Story of Political Corruption and the FBI Informant Who Risked Everything to Expose It **($23.00)**

5. Scoundrels: Defining Political Corruption Through Tales of Political Intrigue in Rhode Island **($20.00)**

6. Monumental Providence: Legends of History in Sculpture, Statuary, Monuments and Memorials **($20.00)**

7. The Essential Guide to Running for Local Office **($15.00)**

8. The Hanging & Redemption of John Gordon: The True Story of Rhode Island's Last Execution **($20.00)**

9. North Providence: A History & The People Who Shaped It **($20.00)**

10. Award Winning Real Estate in a Depressed or Declining Market **($10.00)**

___ (QTY) _____(Title) X _____ (Price) = $ _____

___ (QTY) _____(Title) X _____ (Price) = $ _____

___ (QTY) _____(Title) X _____ (Price) = $ _____

___ (QTY) _____(Title) X _____ (Price) = $ _____

___ (QTY) _____(Title) X _____ (Price) = $ _____

Total for books $_____ + **Postage**** $_____ = **TOTAL COST** $_____

__Postage: Please add $3.00 for the first book and $1.50 for each additional book ordered.__

Payment Method:

___ Personal Check Enclosed (Payable to **M. Caranci Books**)

___ Charge my Credit Card

Name:_____ BILLING ZIP CODE:_____

Visa____ Master Card_____

Card Number:_____ EXP:___/__CSC (3 digit code) _____

Signature:_____

(Order form continues on next page)

<u>Ship My Book To:</u>

Name _____

Street _____

City_____State:_____Zip:_____

Phone _____Email:_____

Special Signing Instructions: IE To Whom do you want the book signed? Do you want me to include a message? Just sign my name? Etc.

_____
_____
_____

<u>MAIL YOUR COMPLETED FORM TO:</u>

Paul F. Caranci

26 East Avenue

North Providence, RI 02911

You may also order using my Email address at municipalheritage@gmail.com

or by calling me at 401-639-4502

Please visit my Website at www.paulcaranci.com